OLFG
Companion
Quick Reference

OLFG Companion
Quick Reference

**For leaders
translating
strategy into action
under pressure,
uncertainty,
and a
narrowing margin.**

Companion to Operational Leader's Field Guide

JAYSON COIL

COGPLEXITI
Flagstaff, Arizona

RELATIONSHIP TO THE PARENT WORK

This volume is a working companion to *Operational Leader's Field Guide: Decision, Adaptation and Performance in Complex Incidents* (Cogplexiti LLC, 2026), and is designed to be used alongside it. The Companion distills the parent work into a field-side reference; it is not a substitute for the parent volume's full treatment of the underlying frameworks. Readers seeking the supporting analysis, evidence, and operational case material should consult the parent Field Guide (ISBN 979-8-9959056-1-5).

REGISTRATION

Registered with the U.S. Copyright Office, Case #1-15150402751.

EDITION INFORMATION

First Edition, 2026 · Pocket Reference Format, 5.25×8
Published by Cogplexiti LLC · Flagstaff, Arizona · jayson@cogplexiti.com
www.cogplexiti.com

DISCLAIMER

The views, frameworks, and recommendations expressed in this publication are those of the author and do not necessarily reflect the official policy or position of the Sedona Fire District, Southwest Incident Management Team 1, the National Wildfire Coordinating Group, the U.S. Forest Service, or any other agency or organization. This document is not doctrine. It is a professional reference informed by operational experience, research, and study.

The guidance in this companion is intended for use by experienced leaders operating in complex environments. It does not replace agency policy, standard operating procedures, or position-specific qualification standards. Leaders are responsible for exercising professional judgment appropriate to their specific operating context.

EDITION INFORMATION

First Edition, April 2026. Quick Reference Format, 5.25 × 8.
Published by Cogplexiti LLC, Flagstaff, Arizona.

jayson@cogplexiti.com
www.cogplexiti.com

"Don't never take a chance you don't have to."

— Major Robert Rogers
Standing Orders, 1759

CONTENTS

Lines That Survive Contact

At some point, you will not remember the framework name.
You will remember the sentence.

That is the purpose of this section. These lines are for the long operational period,
the rushed briefing, the radio conversation, the planning meeting that is drifting, and the
moment when the plan still sounds good but no longer fits the incident. They are short
because the conditions they are meant for do not reward long explanations.

They are not slogans. Each line points back to a larger framework in the Field Guide. Use
them to challenge weak strategy, clarify intent, test assumptions, interrupt drift, or remind
the team that activity is not the same as progress.

The line is what survives contact. The chapter is where the reasoning lives.

ON DECISIONS

— Decision quality is independent of outcome.
The wind shifts. Evaluate the process, not the weather. **(Ch. 4)**

— Hope is not a strategy.
If the plan depends on conditions you do not control, you have a wish. **(Ch. 2)**

— Document the reasoning before the outcome is known.
After the outcome, every decision looks either obvious or stupid. **(Ch. 4)**

— Freezing is a decision.
If you make none, the environment makes one for you. **(Ch. 4)**

ON STRATEGY

— Tactical success that does not advance the strategy is worse than useless.
It burns finite resources and introduces risk. **(Ch. 2)**

— If everything is a priority, nothing is.
Strategy requires choosing what you will not do. **(Ch. 2)**

— Maximum available must exceed minimum required — or the strategy must change.
There is no third option. **(Ch. 2)**

— Strategy is non-linear; tactics are linear.
Different domains. Different thinking. Do not confuse them. **(Ch. 2)**

ON INTENT & COMMUNICATION

— The mission takes precedence over the plan.
Plans are hypotheses. Do not become pregnant with the plan. **(Ch. 1, 5)**

— Intent has to survive five conditions.
If it cannot survive translation, time, and the radio, it has not been communicated. **(Ch. 5)**

— When you deviate, communication requirements increase — they do not decrease.
Deviation without communication is not initiative; it is chaos. **(Ch. 1, 5)**

— Verify with a back-brief.
You are testing landing, not memory. **(Ch. 5)**

Lines That Survive Contact

ON ASSUMPTIONS & CHALLENGE

— Name the load-bearing assumptions — then test them.
If you cannot say which assumption would change your decision, you have not analyzed it. **(Ch. 3)**

— Run the premortem.
Imagine the strategy failed. Why? Then fix that. **(Ch. 3, 6)**

— Someone has explicit license to challenge this.
If no one does, the challenge will arrive from the environment instead. **(Ch. 3)**

ON THE SELF

— Am I thinking clearly?
If the answer is uncertain, the next decision is not yours alone to make. **(Ch. 11)**

— What behavior am I reinforcing?
The team mirrors the leader's behavior, not the leader's words. **(Capstone, Ch. 9)**

— Planning beyond what is knowable is a trap.
Use the time you save to iterate on what you have learned today. **(Ch. 7)**

THE CAPSTONE

Every framework fails if leader behavior contradicts it. The organization believes what leaders tolerate, reward, ignore, and model — before it believes what leaders brief.

The test: when your words and actions diverge, the team treats your actions as the real standard.

This Companion

ANCHOR

A quick-reference pointer, not a substitute for the parent Field Guide.
Use it to find the right framework fast; the reasoning lives in the book.

THREE WAYS TO ENTER

01   **TOPIC REFERENCE**

Use Section III to jump straight to a capability or tool.

Best when you know what you need but cannot remember the framework name.

02   **LIFECYCLE NAVIGATOR**

Use Section II to locate your phase.

Best when the operational rhythm is the question — what cognitive demand dominates right now.

03   **DIAGNOSTIC TOOL**

Use Section IV to translate symptoms into likely causes.

Best when something is wrong but the diagnosis is not yet clear.

NOT A SUBSTITUTE FOR JUDGMENT

Every framework in this book has conditions under which it works and
conditions under which it fails. The leader's job is to know the difference.

The Companion gives you faster access to the framework.
It does not give you faster access to the judgment.

SECTION I

The Operating Environment

What the work demands before any framework helps.

Every framework in this Companion assumes you accept
a particular view of the operating environment. If that
view is wrong, the frameworks fail — not because they
are wrong, but because they were built for a different
kind of problem than the one you are managing.

This section is the premise everything else rests on.

THREE FOUNDATIONS

THE DOMAIN · P. 6

Cynefin. Wildfire is a complex problem, not a complicated
one. The distinction determines whether any approach
has a reasonable chance of working.

THE METHOD · P. 7

SOCOM Design. Appreciate, define, develop — and the
counterintuitive time distribution that makes complex-
domain work different from complicated-domain work.

THE PRINCIPLES · P. 8

Ten operating requirements — not reminders. The
conditions complex environments impose on leaders.
Woven through every chapter that follows.

THE PREMISE

**Match approach to the actual nature
of the problem — not the one you wish it were.**

*If you find yourself returning to this section while reading
later chapters, that is the section doing its job. The
frameworks downstream all depend on it.*

THE CENTRAL DISTINCTION

Complicated vs. Complex

*Most incident management tools were built for one
kind of problem. Wildfire is the other kind.*

<table>
<tr><td>

COMPLICATED
Most planning tools live here.

</td><td>

COMPLEX
Where the work actually lives.

</td></tr>
<tr><td>

CHARACTER

Cause and effect knowable
through expertise.

METHOD

Sense — analyze — respond.
Good practice applies.

PROBLEM

Solvable. Good planning
produces good outcomes.

EXAMPLE

Building an airplane.
A heart transplant.

*If your training came from here,
your defaults will not match the work.*

</td><td>

CHARACTER

Cause and effect coherent
only in retrospect.

METHOD

Probe — sense — respond.
Emergent practice.

PROBLEM

Not solvable. Manageable,
navigable, influenceable.

EXAMPLE

Raising a child.
Managing a wildfire.

*If your work happens here,
your tools must match it.*

</td></tr>
</table>

THE CORE OBSERVATION

Most leaders trained for complicated problems will
apply complicated-domain tools to complex problems
— and produce internally coherent plans that solve

the wrong question, precisely.

WHAT THIS SECTION EQUIPS YOU TO DO

- Recognize the domain you are in before you act on it.
- Apply the method that fits the domain you are in.
- Hold the principles that complex environments impose
  on leaders — whether or not the leader accepts them.

*If you skip this section, every other section is harder.
The downstream content presumes you have absorbed it.*

THE DOMAIN

Cynefin

Match approach to the kind of problem you have.

THE LESSON

Different problems require different approaches.
Misdiagnosing the domain is the most common —
and most consequential — failure.

COMPLEX

Cause and effect coherent
only in retrospect.

Probe — sense — respond.

Distribute decisions to
those closest to the
information.

Wildfire lives here.

COMPLICATED

Cause and effect knowable
through expertise.

Sense — analyze — respond.

Good planning produces
good outcomes. Expertise
reveals the answer.

Most planning tools live here.

CHAOTIC

No discoverable cause-
and-effect. Act decisively.

Act — sense — respond.

Stabilize first. Understand
later. Move out of chaos —
do not stay in it.

First minutes of a blowup.

CLEAR

Cause and effect obvious.
Best-practice exists.

Sense — categorize — respond.

Apply standard procedures
directly. Do not deliberate.

Routine procedural tasks.

DISORDER · WHERE LEADERS DEFAULT

When you cannot tell which domain you are in, the
default is to apply the domain you are most comfortable
with — usually the wrong one.

FAILURE MODE

Applying complicated-domain solutions to complex
problems. Planning your way out of uncertainty.

SOURCE

Kurtz & Snowden, 2003 · Snowden, 2005.

SEE

Page 7 — SOCOM Design

THE METHOD

SOCOM Design

Appreciate, define, develop — in that order, in that ratio.

THE LESSON

In complex environments, most of the work is upstream of the plan. The time distribution is counterintuitive — and that is the point.

APPRECIATE THE CONTEXT   ≈ 65%

Understand the system: terrain, weather, fuel, resources, stakeholders, communities, infrastructure, politics, history.

The system is path-dependent. Your actions will change it — in ways you cannot fully predict.

DEFINE THE PROBLEM   ≈ 25%

Resist the urge to jump to solutions. Sit with uncertainty long enough to understand what you are actually facing —

not what you faced last time. The problem is rarely a single problem. It is a set of interacting problems.

DEVELOP AN APPROACH   ≈ 10%

Logic and sequence of action — not a detailed plan. Held provisionally. The approach will need to change as you

learn what the system will and will not permit. It is the smallest part of the work, not the largest.

FAILURE MODE

Inverting the ratio. Spending 65% of the time on the plan and 10% on understanding what the plan must address.

Plans built on weak appreciation are internally coherent — and externally irrelevant.

DISCIPLINE · WHEN THIS ISN'T WHAT EXPERIENCE PREPARED YOU FOR

Novelty Recognition

Cynefin names the domains. It cannot tell you, in the moment, which domain you are actually in. That move belongs to the leader.

THE LESSON

Notice, in the moment, when the situation is not what experience prepared you for — and reason forward from that recognition rather than from the pattern your experience is offering you.

EXPERTISE WORKS AGAINST IT

Pattern recognition makes experts fast — but cannot verify the pattern still fits. The expert is more vulnerable than the novice, not less. Expertise does not exempt the leader. It increases the obligation.

THE CONVERGENCE OF CONFIDENT ERROR

When the room shares an experience base, it matches the same patterns. Each reading confirms the others. Confidence is not evidence — it is convergence. The room is more confident, and the room is more wrong.

THE THREE MOVES

01 NAME THE NOVELTY — OUT LOUD

The conditions are X, the pattern I am matching is Y, the mismatch is Z. The discipline is communicative, not internal — a private hedge corrects no one.

02 REASON FORWARD FROM THE NOVELTY

Not what did we do last time? but what is actually going on, and what would the right response be with no precedent at all? Draw on principles, not the matching pattern.

03 SLOW THE PLAN WHEN NOVELTY EXCEEDS CONFIDENCE

Not paralysis — calibration. The old tempo runs detailed plans for the wrong conditions. Slow until the situation is understood.

The leader who notices and does not speak has not practiced the discipline. It is not internal. It is communicative.

Ten Principles

Operating requirements, not reminders. Part 1 of 2.

*These principles are woven through every chapter of
this Companion because they must be — they are the
conditions complex environments impose on leaders.*

1   Decision quality is independent of outcomes.

Good decisions can produce bad outcomes through factors beyond your control.
Bad decisions can produce good outcomes through luck. Evaluate the process,
the reasoning, the use of information — not whether the wind shifted.

2   Hope is not strategy.

If your plan depends on conditions you cannot control going your way, you do
not have a strategy. You have a wish. Recognize when hope is masquerading as
strategy — in yourself and in others.

3   Strategy is non-linear. Tactical execution is linear.

These are different domains requiring different thinking. Confusing the two —
applying linear thinking to non-linear problems or treating tactical success
as strategic progress — is one of the most common failures in incident
management.

4   The mission takes precedence over the plan.

Plans are hypotheses. When conditions change and the plan no longer serves the
mission, change the plan. Do not become pregnant with the plan. The plan
exists to serve the mission. The mission does not exist to justify the plan.

5   When you deviate, communication requirements increase.

They do not decrease. Deviation without communication creates divergence
across the organization. Leaders who change direction without communicating
the change, the reason for it, and its implications are not exercising
initiative. They are creating chaos.

THE PRINCIPLES
Ten Principles

Operating requirements, not reminders. Part 2 of 2.

Continued from page 9. Principles 6 through 10 cover iteration, the strategy-tactics link, and resource discipline.

6 Planning beyond what is knowable is a trap.

Detailed planning has value when conditions are predictable. In complex environments, the further you plan into the future, the less your plan resembles what will happen. Plan to the level of detail conditions support — no further. Use the saved time to iterate.

7 Iteration is essential. Clear intent is not optional.

These are not in tension. Clear intent provides the framework within which iteration produces adaptation, not freelancing. Without iteration, intent becomes a rigid script that breaks on contact with reality. Without intent, iteration becomes drift.

8 Tactical success without strategic advance is worse than useless.

It introduces risk and consumes finite resources better committed to actions that advance the strategic end state. Measure outcomes, not outputs. Acres treated and line built are inputs. Strategic effect is the only output that matters.

9 Resources must match the strategy — or the strategy must change.

Maximum available must exceed minimum required. If it does not, the strategy is not viable. Scale it, delay it, or redefine success. A strategy that requires resources you do not have is hope, not strategy.

10 If everything is a priority, nothing is.

Strategy requires explicit choices — including what you will deliberately not do, so what you do choose has the resources and attention it needs to succeed. Strategy is as much about omission as inclusion.

SECTION II

The Incident Lifecycle Arc

Five phases. Each demands something different.

An assignment is not a steady state. Cognitive demands shift as you move through the arc. The leader who applies the right capability at the wrong phase is wasting effort — sometimes catastrophically.

USE THIS SECTION TO —

LOCATE YOURSELF

When uncertain about what to prioritize, ask: where am I in the arc? The answer directs you to the chapters and capabilities that matter most right now.

DIAGNOSE WHY YOU'RE STUCK

If the incident feels stuck, ask: what phase does the team think it's in, and what phase is it actually in? Mismatch is the most common — and most consequential — failure.

NAVIGATE TRANSITIONS

Each phase has exits — forward, backward, or out of the arc. The exit diagnostic at the end of each phase tells you how to recognize when you've actually transitioned.

THE NAVIGATION QUESTION

Where am I in the arc — and what does this phase require of me?

HOW TO READ THE COLOR

Each phase is anchored to a color. Once you recognize the color, you can navigate the section by touch — the top strip on every page tells you which phase you're reading.

- Phase 1 — Assuming Command
- Phase 2 — Establishing Approach
- Phase 3 — Executing & Iterating
- Phase 4 — Recognizing Inflection
- Phase 5 — Transitioning Command

AT A GLANCE

The Five Phases

Each phase, its dominant demand, and its primary failure mode — at a glance. Pages follow.

PHASE 1 Assuming Command *p. 12*

Appreciating the inheritance.

DOMINANT DEMAND

Context appreciation.

> **FAILURE MODE**
> Inheriting the plan without validating the strategy.

PHASE 2 Establishing Approach *p. 15*

From understanding to strategy.

DOMINANT DEMAND

Strategic synthesis.

> **FAILURE MODE**
> Confusing a detailed plan with a sound strategy.

PHASE 3 Executing & Iterating *p. 18*

The operational grind.

DOMINANT DEMAND

Disciplined iteration.

> **FAILURE MODE**
> Executing without iterating. Rhythm as ritual.

PHASE 4 Recognizing Inflection *p. 21*

When the strategy must change.

DOMINANT DEMAND

Intellectual honesty.

> **FAILURE MODE**
> Doubling down on a strategy that no longer fits.

PHASE 5 Transitioning Command *p. 24*

Transferring understanding.

DOMINANT DEMAND

Strategic transfer.

> **FAILURE MODE**
> Transferring information without understanding.

PHASE 1 OF 5

Assuming Command

Appreciating the inheritance.

DOMINANT DEMAND

Context appreciation. Resisting the pressure to act before you understand what you have inherited — and whether it still fits.

USE WHEN

- Just took command.
- New delegation in hand.
- Inherited plan briefed — not yet validated.
- Stakeholders already have expectations of you.
- Resources deployed against the prior approach.

DO

- Read the delegation first.
- Validate the inherited strategy against now.
- Map the stakeholders.
- Name what each one needs.
- Identify the assumptions the prior plan rests on.
- Appreciate before acting.

ASK

- Can I state the inherited strategy in one sentence?
- What conditions has it stopped fitting?
- What was the prior team optimizing for?
- Where does my delegation differ from theirs?

WATCH

- Pressure to execute before appreciating.
- Briefing accepted as context.
- Inherited plan treated as the strategy.
- Stakeholder expectations inherited unexamined.

IF / THEN

If you cannot state the inherited strategy in one sentence, you are still in Phase 1 — regardless of how many operational periods have passed.
Acceptance is not appreciation.

FAILURE MODE

Inheriting the plan without validating the strategy. Treating the transition briefing as the appreciation.

LOG

Delegation of authority · Stakeholder map · One-sentence strategy validation note.

SEE

Pt. I (SOCOM Design) · Ch. 1 (mission command) · Ch. 2 (strategy) · Ch. 5 (intent)

WHAT IT LOOKS LIKE
In the Field

SCENARIO

You take command of an extended attack fire on day six. The outgoing IC briefs you for 40 minutes. The IAP is thorough. The objectives are clear. Crews are in place. The cooperating agency administrator has been working closely with the outgoing team. The weather forecast for tomorrow shows conditions you have not seen this week.

TWO RESPONSES

DONE BADLY	DONE WELL
Accept the IAP. The plan is detailed and the crews are deployed. Pushing back looks like distrust.	**Read the delegation first.** Note where your authority differs from the prior IC's. That is your space.
Treat the briefing as the context. The outgoing IC knows the fire. Their read on conditions becomes yours.	**Take the briefing — then** appreciate. Spend the first hours observing, not directing. The fire teaches you what the briefing can't.
Inherit the stakeholder relationships. The agency administrator already trusts the team. You will continue the rapport.	**Re-establish the stakeholder** relationships on your terms. Trust is not transferable. It is earned each time.
Execute against tomorrow's conditions using yesterday's assumptions. The plan was built for the weather you no longer have.	**Validate the plan against** tomorrow. State the inherited strategy in one sentence. Test whether it still fits the forecast.

SELF-AUDIT · THREE QUESTIONS

1 Can I state the inherited strategy in one sentence — and the conditions under which it stops fitting?

2 Have I read my delegation — or am I assuming it matches my predecessor's?

3 Am I executing tomorrow's plan against yesterday's conditions — or have I tested the match?

If any answer is no, you are still in Phase 1.

HOW TO KNOW YOU'VE
Left This Phase

*Phases overlap. Transitions are rarely announced. You
read them through observable conditions, not the calendar.*

EXIT PATHWAY · 1 OF 1
Phase 1 → Phase 2
Establishing Approach

SIGNPOSTS · YOU CAN EXIT WHEN

• You can state the inherited strategy in one sentence —
and the conditions under which it stops fitting.

• Your delegation of authority is read, acknowledged,
and you know where it differs from your predecessor's.

• Your stakeholder map is built — not inherited.

TRANSITION RISK

Phase 2 demands strategic synthesis — taking your
appreciation and producing a coherent approach
with defined ends, ways, means, and risk.

If you exit Phase 1 with incomplete appreciation,
Phase 2 produces a plan, not a strategy.

COGNITIVE SHIFT REQUIRED

Phase 1: receptive thinking. Take in, sit with, resist
the pressure to act. Comfort with not yet knowing.

Phase 2: generative thinking. Synthesize, choose,
commit to a defended approach. Comfort with
deciding under uncertainty.

YOU HAVEN'T ACTUALLY EXITED IF —

You're building Phase 2's strategy from the inherited
plan's assumptions instead of your own appreciation.

WHAT THIS PHASE BOUGHT YOU

You carry four things into Phase 2 that the prior team's
briefing alone could not have given you:

• A validated one-sentence read of the strategy.
• An owned delegation of authority.
• A stakeholder map built on your own contact.
• The assumptions the prior plan rests on — named.

PHASE 2 OF 5

Establishing Approach

From understanding to strategy.

DOMINANT DEMAND

Strategic synthesis. Translating your appreciation into a coherent approach with defined ends, ways, means, and risk.

USE WHEN

- Appreciation is complete.
- You can state the problem, not just the symptoms.
- The inherited strategy has been validated or rejected.
- You are ready to commit to an approach — and defend the tradeoffs it implies.

DO

- Define ends, ways, means, and risk explicitly.
- Run a Key Assumptions Check before committing.
- Run a premortem. Identify the failure modes now.
- Build the contingency architecture, not just plans.

ASK

- Is this a strategy, or is it a plan dressed as one?
- What must be true for this approach to work?
- What decision points have I named in advance?
- Which assumptions, if they fail, change everything?

WATCH

- Tactical detail substituting for strategic logic.
- Consensus mistaken for rigor.
- Pressure to brief before the assumptions are tested.
- An approach that survives only one set of conditions.

IF / THEN

If you cannot articulate the theory of action — the link between what you do and what you achieve — what you have is a plan, not a strategy.
A plan tells you what. A strategy tells you why.

FAILURE MODE

Jumping to execution before the strategy is coherent. Confusing a detailed plan with a sound strategy.

LOG

Strategy statement · Assumptions register · Decision points · Triggers for adaptation.

SEE

Ch. 2 (ISAP, operational art) · Ch. 3 (KAC, premortem) · Ch. 5 (ITPE) · Ch. 7 (contingency)

WHAT IT LOOKS LIKE

In the Field

SCENARIO

Appreciation is complete. The fire is in a fuel type your team knows, but the values at risk include a community your team does not. Resources are adequate for the forecast — not for the forecast plus a 20% degradation. Your delegation gives wide latitude. The agency expects a strategy by tomorrow's planning meeting.

TWO RESPONSES

DONE BADLY	DONE WELL
Write objectives. Six bullets covering the fire, the community, and aviation. Brief them at the meeting.	**Write the theory of action.** One paragraph: how the approach produces the end state, with what tradeoffs.
Skip the assumptions check. The fuel type is familiar. The team has done this before. Move fast.	**Run the assumptions check.** Familiarity is not a substitute. Name what must be true. Identify what could break it.
Treat contingency as a plan. "If conditions degrade, we reassess." Specific triggers are not identified.	**Build contingency triggers.** Specific observable conditions, named actions, named owners, named decision-makers.
Plan to the forecast. Resources match expected conditions. Confidence is high. The 20% degradation scenario remains unbuilt.	**Plan for forecast plus 20%.** Identify the resources, the trigger, and the decision-maker before the conditions arrive.

SELF-AUDIT · THREE QUESTIONS

1 Can I state the theory of action — the link between what we do and what we achieve — in one paragraph?

2 Have I named the assumptions that, if they fail, change the strategy — not just the plan?

3 Are my contingencies triggered by observable conditions — or by someone noticing in time?

If any answer is no, your strategy is incomplete.

HOW TO KNOW YOU'VE
Left This Phase

Phase 2 has two exits — forward to execution, or back if appreciation gaps surface during synthesis.

EXIT PATHWAY · 1 OF 2 · FORWARD
Phase 2 → Phase 3
Executing & Iterating

SIGNPOSTS
- Strategy communicated through ITPE / DTOF to all levels.
- Decision points and triggers identified for monitoring.
- Contingency architecture in place — not just plans.

If divisions cannot restate the strategy, it has not transitioned.

COGNITIVE SHIFT REQUIRED

Phase 2: generative thinking. Build the strategy.
Phase 3: iterative thinking. Test the strategy daily against conditions. The plan is a hypothesis, not a commitment.

EXIT PATHWAY · 2 OF 2 · BACKWARD
Phase 2 ← Phase 1
Re-appreciate

SIGNPOSTS — YOU NEED TO GO BACK WHEN
- Synthesis keeps stalling on questions you can't answer.
- You're discovering load-bearing facts you should have surfaced during appreciation.

Going back is not a failure — pretending you don't need to is.

WHAT GOING BACK COSTS — AND SAVES

Costs: time, momentum, possibly credibility.
Saves: a strategy that survives contact with conditions you would have otherwise discovered in Phase 3 or 4.

YOU HAVEN'T ACTUALLY EXITED IF —

You've briefed objectives without communicating intent.
Divisions can recite the plan but cannot explain why.

WHAT THIS PHASE BOUGHT YOU

You carry five things into Phase 3 that no plan, however detailed, could supply on its own:

- A defensible theory of action.
- Named, load-bearing assumptions — and their owners.
- Decision points identified in advance, not in hindsight.
- Contingency triggers tied to observable conditions.
- Intent that has been cascaded through ITPE / DTOF.

PHASE 3 OF 5

Executing & Iterating

The operational grind.

DOMINANT DEMAND

Disciplined execution with continuous iteration.
Maintaining strategic coherence while adapting
every operational period.

USE WHEN

- Strategy is briefed and cascaded.
- Daily rhythm is running: pre-ops, midday, post-ops.
- Conditions are within the range the strategy was designed for.
- Iteration is the work.

DO

- Hold the daily rhythm as discipline, not ritual.
- Monitor your assumptions. Treat them as provisional.
- Close every loop. Track every tasking to outcome.
- Protect cognitive readiness as fatigue accumulates.

ASK

- What did we learn today that the plan didn't predict?
- Are we iterating, or just executing the same plan?
- Which assumptions have been tested? Which haven't?
- Is the team's cognitive capacity degrading?

WATCH

- Activity confused with progress.
- Daily rhythm hardening into ceremony.
- Reports describing the plan rather than the field.
- Fatigue worn as a badge rather than a warning.

IF / THEN

If you have run the same plan three days without
refining it, you are no longer iterating — you are
executing past the point where the plan still fits.
Activity is not adaptation.

FAILURE MODE

Executing without iterating. Allowing rhythm to
become ritual. Measuring activity, not strategic effect.

LOG

Daily SAPPER · Assumption updates ·
Decision log · Trigger status.

SEE

Ch. 4 (decision quality) · Ch. 5 (rhythm,
closing loops) · Ch. 7 (iteration) · Ch. 11 (fatigue)

WHAT IT LOOKS LIKE

In the Field

SCENARIO

Day nine. The strategy is holding. Crews are tired but competent. Division supervisors are running the daily rhythm. Today's post-ops report from Division Z notes fire behavior at the upper edge of forecast. The IMET flags a chance of single-digit RH and downsloping winds two operational periods out.

TWO RESPONSES

DONE BADLY	DONE WELL
Run today's plan. The plan is working. Crews are on task. Repeating yesterday's success is the safe move.	**Refine today's plan.** Working does not mean optimal. Where can iteration buy back margin before the weather arrives?
Note the IMET briefing. Acknowledge the upcoming conditions. Add a line to tomorrow's IAP.	**Test the assumption now.** Single-digit RH was a load-bearing assumption. Is the contingency still feasible?
Brief tomorrow as routine. Crews are tired. Don't add complexity. Address the weather when it arrives.	**Pre-activate the contingency.** Position resources, brief the trigger, name the decision-maker. Don't wait for the trigger to act on the trigger.
Treat the post-ops as information, not signal. Division Z's report becomes a paragraph in the morning briefing.	**Treat the post-ops as signal.** Division Z is reading the future. Move that signal up the chain immediately.

SELF-AUDIT · THREE QUESTIONS

1. What did today teach us that the strategy didn't predict — and what did we change as a result?

2. Which load-bearing assumption have I tested most recently? Which have I quietly stopped testing?

3. Am I making decisions, or am I confirming the decisions I made on day two?

If any answer is no, the rhythm has become ritual.

HOW TO KNOW YOU'VE

Left This Phase

Phase 3 has three exits — the strategy stops fitting, the strategy concludes within scope, or the strategy was wrong.

EXIT PATHWAY · 1 OF 3 · INFLECTION
Phase 3 → Phase 4
Recognizing Inflection

SIGNPOSTS · COGNITIVE SHIFT

• Fire behavior, resource picture, or stakeholder priorities have shifted outside the strategy's design envelope.
• Load-bearing assumptions have failed — not edge cases.
• Iteration cannot recover the gap. Strategy must change.

Cognitive shift: from iteration to honest reassessment.
The cost of not adapting is higher than the cost of changing.

EXIT PATHWAY · 2 OF 3 · CONCLUSION
Phase 3 → Phase 5
Transitioning Command

SIGNPOSTS · COGNITIVE SHIFT

• End state conditions are within reach with current resources and approach.
• Transition window is opening — incoming team identified.
• Learning during execution must now be made transferable.

Cognitive shift: from operating to packaging — for someone else to inherit and continue.

EXIT PATHWAY · 3 OF 3 · BACKWARD
Phase 3 ← Phase 2
Re-establish Strategy

DISTINCTION FROM PATHWAY 1

Pathway 1: the strategy fit the conditions, but conditions changed. Adapt the strategy to new conditions.

Pathway 3: the strategy never fit the conditions you actually had. Rebuild the strategy on accurate appreciation

This is the hardest exit. The honest one.

YOU HAVEN'T ACTUALLY EXITED IF —

You're still iterating tactics on a strategy that no longer fits — or that never fit. Iteration is not a substitute for change.

PHASE 4 OF 5

Recognizing Inflection

When the strategy must change.

DOMINANT DEMAND

Intellectual honesty and adaptive leadership.
Recognizing the current approach is no longer viable
— and having the discipline to change it.

USE WHEN

• Fire behavior, conditions,
or resource picture has
shifted outside the strategy.
• Load-bearing assumptions
have failed.
• Iteration cannot recover.
• Cost of continuing is
rising. Cost of changing is
not.

DO

• Name the inflection
explicitly. Out loud.
• Distinguish failing execution
from a failing strategy.
• Re-synchronize stakeholders
to the new approach.
• Accept the cost of change.
It is lower than the cost
of not.

ASK

• Am I treating new conditions
as noise around the strategy
— or as signal against it?
• What evidence am I
discounting because it
threatens the current plan?
• Who on my team has been
trying to tell me this?

WATCH

• Attributing failure to
conditions, not approach.
• Doubling resources against
the same strategy.
• Hoping conditions will
improve.
• Counting the sunk cost
of the current approach.

IF / THEN

If you find yourself defending the strategy against
the field's reports rather than updating it from them,
the inflection has already happened — and you are late.
Hope is not strategy.

FAILURE MODE

Doubling down on a strategy that no longer fits.
Hoping rather than adapting.

LOG

Inflection statement · Strategy revision ·
Stakeholder re-sync log · Decision rationale.

SEE

Ch. 2 (strategic adaptation) · Ch. 3 (red
teaming) · Ch. 4 (epistemic humility) · Ch. 7

WHAT IT LOOKS LIKE
In the Field

SCENARIO

Day twelve. The containment strategy has held for nine days. Yesterday a slop-over breached your primary control line. Today the IMET is briefing a multi-day pattern shift. Your resources are committed. The agency administrator just told the press the fire will be contained within seven days.

TWO RESPONSES

DONE BADLY	DONE WELL
Reinforce the line. Order more crews. Add aviation. The strategy is working — yesterday was a bad day.	**Name the inflection.** Out loud, to the team: "The containment strategy no longer fits the conditions we now have."
Defer the IMET briefing. Acknowledge the forecast. Set it aside for tomorrow's planning meeting.	**Treat the IMET as the brief.** The forecast is the strategic input, not an addendum. Rebuild around it.
Stay aligned with the AA. The seven-day timeline is public. Walking it back will damage credibility. Push through.	**Re-sync the AA immediately.** Surprise destroys trust faster than honest reassessment. Update the timeline before the news does.
Wait for the next data point. One bad day is not a pattern. Let tomorrow tell us whether the strategy still fits.	**Decide on evidence available.** Waiting for confirmation that the strategy has failed is the definition of being late.

SELF-AUDIT · THREE QUESTIONS

1 Am I treating bad news as noise around the strategy — or as signal against it?

2 What am I adding resources to instead of changing — and what does that say about my read?

3 Who has been trying to tell me the strategy has stopped working — and why am I not hearing it?

If you cannot answer all three honestly, you have not yet named the inflection.

HOW TO KNOW YOU'VE
Left This Phase

Phase 4 has two exits — transition the operation to a new team, or rebuild the strategy and re-enter execution.

EXIT PATHWAY · 1 OF 2 · TRANSITION OUT
Phase 4 → Phase 5
Transitioning Command

SIGNPOSTS

• The inflection demands more than this team can deliver in the time available — a Type 1 transition, or out.
• Your team's capacity, fatigue state, or scope-fit no longer matches what the new conditions require.

COGNITIVE SHIFT

From adapting the operation to packaging it for someone else. The hardest part is staying engaged through transition after you've decided the operation needs a different team.

EXIT PATHWAY · 2 OF 2 · NEW STRATEGY
Phase 4 ← Phase 2
Rebuild Approach

SIGNPOSTS

• The inflection is within this team's capacity to rebuild around.
• New conditions have been appreciated — the gap was strategy-shaped, not capacity-shaped.

Returning to Phase 2 is the work, not the surrender.

WHAT YOU CARRY BACK

Updated appreciation, learned during execution. Tested assumptions — including the ones that failed. A team that knows the conditions in ways the inherited plan never did.

YOU HAVEN'T ACTUALLY EXITED IF —

You've named the inflection in your head but not to your team, your AA, or your strategy on the IAP.

WHAT THIS PHASE BOUGHT YOU

Whichever exit you took, you carry forward what only an honest inflection produces:

• A named, acknowledged mismatch — not a hidden one.
• Stakeholders re-synchronized to ground truth.
• A team that watched you tell the truth under pressure.
• An accurate record of why the change was made — for whoever inherits the operation next.

PHASE 5 OF 5

Transitioning Command

Transferring understanding, not just information.

DOMINANT DEMAND

Ensuring the strategic reasoning — not just the plan, the documents, and the resource list — transfers to the next entity.

USE WHEN

- Transition window has opened or been triggered.
- Incoming team identified.
- Operation is concluding, or scope is shifting to a different team type.
- Learning during execution is at risk of being lost.

DO

- Transfer the reasoning, not just the plan.
- Document the assumptions that must continue to hold.
- Walk the line with the incoming leader.
- Stay engaged until command is formally transferred.

ASK

- Does the incoming team know why I built this strategy — not just what it is?
- What did we learn that the documents don't show?
- What conditions would require them to change it?

WATCH

- Briefing treated as the transition.
- Disengagement before command is transferred.
- Documents handed over without context.
- Insights left in the heads of departing team members.

IF / THEN

If the incoming team can recite your plan but cannot articulate the reasoning behind it, you have transferred information — not understanding.

Documents are a record, not a transfer.

FAILURE MODE

Transferring information without transferring understanding. Disengaging before command transfers.

LOG

Strategic reasoning narrative · Open decisions · Active assumptions · Transferred lessons.

SEE

Ch. 2 (strategic framework for transfer) · Ch. 5 (intent) · Ch. 8 (learning) · Ch. 10

WHAT IT LOOKS LIKE

In the Field

Day fourteen. Conditions are stabilizing. The incoming Type 2 team is in-briefing tomorrow. Your IAP is current. Three assumptions you made on day three have shaped every decision since — and two of them are not in any document. The agency administrator and the affected community have learned to read you. Not your replacement.

TWO RESPONSES

DONE BADLY

Brief from the IAP.
Walk through the current plan. The documents capture the operation — they will fill in the rest.

Leave the assumptions silent.
They're internal. They've worked. The new team will develop their own read on the conditions.

Hand over the relationships.
Introduce the AA at the in-brief. They'll figure it out.

Disengage after the brief.
Command transfers at noon. Demob tomorrow. The new team has the documents and the contacts.

DONE WELL

Brief from the reasoning.
Why this strategy and not the alternatives. What we tried and stopped. Why we kept going.

Name the assumptions.
Write them down. Mark the ones that must continue to hold. Mark the ones already under strain.

Walk the relationships in.
Bring the new IC to the AA personally. Brief them together. Vouch — then step back.

Stay engaged through demob.
Be reachable. The first 48 hours after transfer is when the questions arrive.

SELF-AUDIT · THREE QUESTIONS

1. Can the incoming team articulate why I made the strategy — not just what it is?

2. Are the assumptions that must continue to hold named — on paper, not in someone's memory?

3. Have I stayed engaged — or did I check out at the briefing and call the work done?

If any answer is no, the transition is not complete.

HOW TO KNOW YOU'VE

Left the Arc

Phase 5 has one exit — out of the arc entirely. The operation continues without you, or it concludes.

EXIT PATHWAY · 1 OF 1 · OUT OF THE ARC
Phase 5 → Out
Demobilization / Next Team

SIGNPOSTS

• Command formally transferred. Authority no longer yours.
• Strategic reasoning has landed — the incoming team can defend the strategy in their own words.
• Open decisions, active assumptions, and contingency triggers are documented and acknowledged.

THE 48-HOUR ENGAGEMENT WINDOW

Formal transfer is not the end of your engagement. The incoming team will discover what the documents didn't capture in the first 48 hours. Be reachable. Answer honestly. Do not second-guess from outside the system.

COGNITIVE SHIFT

From operator to advisor. The decisions are no longer yours to make. Your job is to make the new team's decisions easier to make well.

YOU HAVEN'T ACTUALLY EXITED IF —

Command transferred but reasoning did not. The new team has a plan they will execute on faith — or replace.

WHAT THIS PHASE BOUGHT YOU

You leave the arc carrying what only a complete transition produces:

• An operation that continues without you and is no worse for it.
• Lessons captured in transferable form, not just memory.
• Stakeholder relationships handed off, not abandoned.
• A team that learned what good transition looks like — and will hand off the same way next time.

The arc closes here.
For the next leader, it begins again at Phase 1.

COMPARING THE PHASES

Side by Side

What each phase demands, produces, and fails on.
Read horizontally to compare phases. Read vertically to follow one.

	PHASE 1 Assuming	PHASE 2 Establishing	PHASE 3 Executing	PHASE 4 Recognizing	PHASE 5 Transitioning
DEMANDS *What the phase requires of the leader.*					
	Receptive thinking. Appreciation over action. Comfort with not yet knowing.	Generative thinking. Synthesize appreciation into a defended approach.	Iterative thinking. Test the plan daily. Treat it as a hypothesis, not a contract.	Intellectual honesty. Read bad news as signal, not noise.	Strategic transfer. Teach the reasoning, not just the plan.
PRODUCES *What the leader carries forward if the phase is done well.*					
	A validated read of inherited strategy. Stakeholder map. Owned delegation.	Defensible theory of action. Named assumptions. Contingency architecture.	Updated assumptions. Closed loops. A team that learns daily.	Acknowledged mismatch. Stakeholders re-synchronized. Honest record.	An operation that continues without you and is no worse for it.
FAILS WHEN *The dominant failure mode of the phase.*					
	The briefing is treated as the appreciation. The plan is inherited unread.	Tactical detail substitutes for strategic logic. A plan is mistaken for a strategy.	Rhythm becomes ritual. The plan is executed past the point it still fits.	Failure attributed to conditions, not approach. Hoping rather than adapting.	Documents handed over without reasoning. The team departs before the work is done.

WHEN THE CALENDAR LIES
Reading the Drift

The most consequential failure in this section is phase mismatch: thinking you're in one phase while the conditions are demanding another.

THE DIAGNOSTIC QUESTION

What phase does the team think it's in — and what phase is it actually in?

FOUR COMMON DRIFT PATTERNS

THINKS IT'S IN	VS.	ACTUALLY IN
PHASE 3	→	PHASE 1

SYMPTOM

Team is executing aggressively but keeps returning to foundational questions about what the operation is for.

WHAT TO DO

Stop. Appreciation is incomplete. Go back to Phase 1 before more resources are committed.

THINKS IT'S IN	VS.	ACTUALLY IN
PHASE 3	→	PHASE 4

SYMPTOM

Iteration is producing diminishing returns. Bad news accumulates. Team works harder on a plan that no longer fits.

WHAT TO DO

Name the inflection. Move to Phase 4. Cost of continuing now exceeds cost of changing.

THINKS IT'S IN	VS.	ACTUALLY IN
PHASE 2	→	PHASE 3

SYMPTOM

Team keeps refining the plan but never commits. Synthesis stalls. Confidence is high; action is not.

WHAT TO DO

Commit. Phase 2 is over. Plan will not be perfect. Move to Phase 3 and iterate from there.

THINKS IT'S IN	VS.	ACTUALLY IN
PHASE 4	→	PHASE 5

SYMPTOM

The inflection demands a team that is not yours. You're rebuilding strategy for someone else to execute.

WHAT TO DO

Move to Phase 5. Transfer the work. Don't rebuild for an operation you won't run.

THE CORE MOVE

Phases do not announce themselves. The calendar does not tell you which phase you are in. The conditions do.

Your job is to read them — before the team pays the cost of delay.

SEE ALSO

Each phase's exit diagnostic (pages 14, 17, 20, 23, 26) covers transitions between specific phases. Use this page for cross-arc drift.

CHAPTER 1 OF 11

Mission Command

Decentralized execution with centralized intent.

Mission command is not a leadership style or a delegation preference. It is a deliberate structural choice about where decisions are made, how authority is distributed, and what the relationship between leader and subordinate must look like for an organization to function in complex environments.

It is widely invoked. It is rarely practiced.

IN THIS CHAPTER

Prerequisites for Mission Command
Trust, clear intent, shared understanding, competence — the four conditions without which mission command is a label, not a practice.

What It Is, What It Is Not
Six recognizable failure modes. The shortcut diagnostics.

ITPE — Intent, Task, Purpose, End State
The communication structure that translates direction into action.

Decision Space
The room between constraint and freedom. Half of the contract.

Decision Elevation Thresholds
The conditions that return authority upward. The other half.

Inside the Space · Across the Threshold
Two distinct modes of action — and how to know which one applies.

Leader-Task Fit Check
Five-dimension assignment diagnostic before space is calibrated.

THE CHAPTER'S CLAIM

Mission command is a system of paired disciplines — never just one. Each tool in this chapter has a counterpart. *Skip the counterpart and you have half a contract.*

PARENT REFERENCE
OLFG Ch. 1, pages 37–58.

RELATED CHAPTERS
Ch. 5 (Communication & Intent) ·
Ch. 9 (Team Cohesion)

TOOL · THE FOUR PRECONDITIONS

Prerequisites

THE LESSON

Mission command does not work by declaration. Four conditions must be deliberately built and maintained. Without them, execution degrades into freelancing or inertia.

T TRUST

The binding element. Built on shared values, demonstrated competence, consistent behavior over time. Operates in two dimensions — human and organizational. Trust takes time to build and can be destroyed in a single act. There is no workaround for absent trust.

I CLEAR INTENT

Communicates what to achieve, why it matters, and the constraints — without prescribing methods. Enables adaptation; does not force it. If your division supervisors cannot state your intent in their own words, your intent has not been communicated — it has been transmitted.

S SHARED UNDERSTANDING

Not the same as shared information. Subordinates and the leader operate from the same picture of the situation, the strategy, and what success looks like. Built through dialogue, not information transfer. The picture must be tested, not assumed.

C COMPETENCE

Delegating authority to leaders without the capability to exercise it produces chaos — not empowerment. Competence must be matched to the decision space delegated. The most common error: assuming competence at one level transfers automatically to the next.

Trust is the binding element. Without it, none of the others function.

WHAT IT IS NOT

Six Failure Modes

*Mission command is widely invoked and rarely practiced.
The most common failures are recognizable. Name them
before they name you.*

DIRECTIVE CONTROL

Telling people what to do AND how to do it.
When you prescribe the method, you own the
adequacy of that method in conditions you may
not fully understand. This is not mission
command. It is directive control wearing the
label.

ABDICATION

Giving people freedom to do whatever they want.
Freedom without intent, constraints, or
elevation thresholds is not delegation — it is
abandonment. Subordinates will fill the vacuum
with their own assumptions. The results will
not align.

REFLEXIVE PUSH-DOWN

Pushing every decision to the lowest level,
regardless of context. Decision space must be
calibrated to the consequence and to the
competence available. A decision that requires
incident-level information cannot be made well
at the division level.

DECLARED BY EMAIL

Announcing mission command in a values
statement, a memo, or a wall poster. Mission
command is built through repeated demonstration,
not pronouncement. The team reads what leaders
tolerate, reward, and model — not what leaders
brief.

DISGUISED CENTRALIZATION

Centralized control labeled as coordination.
Frequent check-ins, mandatory permissions, and
approval gates that suppress initiative while
preserving the rhetoric of decentralization. The
operation pauses every time the leader is not
available.

DIFFUSED ACCOUNTABILITY

"We all decided." Accountability becomes a
collective fog. No one owns the call; no one
owns the consequence. Disciplined initiative
requires both individual authority and
individual responsibility — distributed, not
diffused.

THE ABSENCE TEST

What happens when you step away? If the operation pauses,
mission command does not exist — whatever the briefing says.

ITPE

Intent · Task · Purpose · End State.

THE LESSON

Every assignment must carry four elements. The absence
of any one degrades the value of the others.

I · INTENT

Why this matters to the larger strategy. The reason that survives when
the plan does not. Intent is what enables a subordinate to make sound
calls when conditions change in ways the plan didn't anticipate.

T · TASK

What to accomplish. Specific enough to act on, broad enough to permit
adaptation in execution. The task is what — not how. Prescribing the
method converts mission command into directive control.

P · PURPOSE

How this task connects to the next echelon's mission. The link that
lets a subordinate make sound calls when the task changes. A task
without a purpose is an instruction that cannot be adapted.

E · END STATE

What success looks like — observable, measurable. The condition that
tells the field leader the assignment is complete. A purpose without
an end state is a direction without a destination.

VERIFY

Have the receiver restate ITPE in their own words. You are testing
landing, not memory. See p. 37 for the back-brief in detail.

TOOL · CALIBRATING AUTHORITY

Decision Space

The room between constraint and freedom.

WHAT IT IS

The room between the constraints you define and the freedom you delegate. Decision space defines what falls within delegated authority — without seeking approval.

TWO CALIBRATION FAILURES

TOO NARROW

Subordinates depend on you for every adjustment.

Your decision cycle becomes the bottleneck for the whole operation. The team waits for permission to adapt to conditions you cannot see.

SYMPTOMS

• Routine adjustments stall pending your input.
• You are the constraint on tempo.

TOO WIDE

Decisions diverge from the strategy without your awareness.

Without sufficient competence or shared understanding, subordinates make decisions that solve local problems while undermining the strategic intent.

SYMPTOMS

• Coordination friction increases.
• Outcomes don't aggregate to strategy.

CALIBRATE TO

• **The person.** Their experience, judgment, risk tolerance, and ability to communicate when they reach the edge of their space.

• **The consequence.** What failure costs — and what recovery requires.

• **The team's maturity.** Adjust as competence and trust accumulate.

HALF OF THE CONTRACT

Decision space without elevation thresholds is freelancing. Decision space communicates what is delegated. Elevation thresholds communicate what is not. See next page.

Implied decision space is friction, not freedom.

Elevation Thresholds

The other half of the contract.

WHAT A THRESHOLD IS

A future condition or event that, if it occurs, requires the subordinate leader to inform the next echelon before committing to action. Specific. Observable. Tied to the decision it changes.

COMMON THRESHOLDS

Pre-define these in delegation. Communicate them explicitly during briefing.

- A division is about to commit its last available structure protection group.
- A primary control feature is breached, or projected to be breached.
- An evacuation trigger is reached earlier than the model projected.
- A medevac, entrapment, serious injury, or significant near-miss occurs.
- A firing operation is about to exceed the approved scope.
- A scarce shared resource — aviation, REMS, dozer, task force — is about to be redirected.
- Conditions invalidate a documented planning assumption.

Each of these changes the calculus the senior leader used to delegate the authority in the first place. None should be decided alone.

THE THRESHOLD TEST

After delivering intent, ask the receiving leader two questions:

1. What are you authorized to decide without asking?

2. What conditions, if they emerge, require you to report before deciding?

If they cannot answer the second crisply, the thresholds were not communicated — even if you believe they were briefed.

VAGUE LANGUAGE DEFEATS THE PURPOSE

"If things get bad" is not a threshold. "If suppression difficulty shifts from 4 to 6 or higher, hold position and report" is.

DIAGRAM · TWO MODES

Inside & Across

Two distinct categories of moment.

The same operation generates two distinct categories of moment. The categories are not gradients on a continuum. They are different modes — and they demand different action.

INSIDE THE SPACE
Act. Report as part of normal rhythm.

WHAT THIS LOOKS LIKE

Tactical adaptation within the assignment.
Adjusting sequence, position, or method to preserve intent under changing conditions.

Resource shifts within the division.
Reallocating crews, engines, or aviation within your area without drawing from others.

Sequencing changes that preserve intent.
Doing the same work in a different order when conditions favor a different sequence.

Routine deviations that do not change the strategic picture.
Small adjustments that the senior leader does not need to know in real time.

THE MODE
Decide. Act. Report on rhythm.
Initiative is the default disposition.
Hesitation costs more than action.

ACROSS THE THRESHOLD
Hold. Report. Wait for guidance.

WHAT THIS LOOKS LIKE

Last reserve about to be committed.
A structure group, a strike team, an aviation asset — when there is no second option.

Control feature compromised or projected.
The primary line, the road, the ridge that the strategy depends on.

Evacuation trigger reached early.
The model said tomorrow. The conditions are saying now.

Entrapment, near-miss, medevac.
Any event that changes the safety picture or requires command-level resourcing.

Documented assumption invalidated.
A condition the plan rested on no longer holds.

THE MODE
Hold. Report. Wait.
Hesitation is the discipline.

THE LEADER'S TASK

Define both columns. Communicate them explicitly.
The leader who has defined only one column has communicated half a contract.

TOOL · BEFORE SPACE IS CALIBRATED

Leader-Task Fit

Five dimensions. Three ratings. One question.

THE LESSON

Calibrating decision space presumes the right person was assigned. Before space is calibrated, the assignment must fit.

DIMENSION	GREEN	YELLOW	RED
CAPABILITY *Skills to execute*	Proven in similar task and conditions	Capable with periodic check-in	Unproven, miscast, or capability gap
CAPACITY *Bandwidth available*	Has bandwidth for this assignment	Competing priorities, manageable	Already at or beyond saturation
CONTEXT *Bigger-picture sight*	Sees how task connects upward	Needs framing to see connection	Lacks the bigger picture
CONSEQUENCE *Stakes of failure*	Failure recoverable in period	Failure has operational cost	Failure high-consequence
SUPERVISION *Support required*	Minimal — periodic verification	Scheduled check-ins required	Close oversight throughout

THE MOST COMMON FAILURE

The high performer rated GREEN on capability and reflexively assigned every difficult task. Capability is accurate. Capacity is not — because the question was never asked. Over time, the high performer absorbs assignments until they fail at one of them.

The fit check exists to make assignment decisions deliberate — not to diagnose them after they fail.

The Back-Brief

Testing whether intent landed — before it matters.

THE LESSON

The brief-back cycle is not a formality. It is how intent gets unpacked into action at the right level — and how you find misalignment before it becomes field friction.

WHAT AN EFFECTIVE BACK-BRIEF CONTAINS

The receiving leader's translation — in their own words — not a repeat.

THE FOUR THINGS YOU ARE TESTING

Task — what they understand they are being asked to do.

Purpose — why the task matters and how it connects upward.

End State — what success looks like in observable terms.

Plus: any assumptions or constraints they're carrying that you didn't intend.

IF THE BACK-BRIEF REVEALS A GAP

Treat it as information about your intent — its clarity, specificity, or framing — not as the subordinate's failure.

Fix the intent before they leave the briefing.
Not after the plan unravels in the field.

The Absence Test

Run when you cannot be present.

THE QUESTION

What happens when you are not present?

Mission command works when subordinates can act correctly without you. If the operation pauses every time you step away, mission command does not exist — whatever you brief.

THE PAIRED DISCIPLINES

Back-brief tests landing. Absence test tests durability.
Without both, you have communicated to yourself.

CHAPTER CLOSE · DIAGNOSTIC PATTERNS

Watch For

When mission command is failing in your operation.

The diagnostic patterns below are not the failure modes themselves. They are the signals the operation produces when a failure mode is already active — and how to find which one.

PATTERN · TEMPO COLLAPSE

The operation gets slower under pressure, not faster.

- Routine adaptations require your approval.
- Division supervisors check in for matters within their delegation.
- Your inbox is the bottleneck on tempo.
- Field calls wait until you're available.

Diagnosis: Decision space too narrow, or trust insufficient.
First test: Run the absence test. See what continues.

PATTERN · COHERENCE DRIFT

Divisions are active. The strategy is not.

- Three division supervisors describe the strategy three different ways.
- Tactical outcomes don't aggregate toward strategic ends.
- Resources flow to whatever feels urgent locally.
- Coordination friction is rising daily.

Diagnosis: Intent did not land. Shared understanding absent.
First test: Back-brief three division supervisors separately.

PATTERN · ACCOUNTABILITY FOG

When something goes wrong, no one can say who decided.

- Post-event reconstruction reveals no clear decision owner.
- Decisions described as "we" — never as "I."
- Threshold conditions were missed because no one was watching.
- Learning is generic; accountability is diffuse.

Diagnosis: Decision space and thresholds not explicitly assigned.
First test: Reconstruct a recent decision. Who was authorized?

SEE ALSO

Section IV (Diagnostic Index) maps these patterns to the broader capabilities they implicate. Most mission-command failures cascade into Ch. 5 (Communication) and Ch. 9 (Team Cohesion) territory.

CHAPTER 2 OF 11

Strategic Thinking

Ends, ways, means, risk — and the art that connects them.

Strategy is a theory of action — a coherent account of what you are trying to achieve, how you intend to achieve it, what you will commit to do it, and what you are willing to risk in the doing.

It is widely confused with planning. They are not the same.

IN THIS CHAPTER

Strategy vs. Plan vs. Pronouncement
Four things people call strategy — only one of them is.

Ends · Ways · Means · Risk
The four-element structure. Missing any one means you have a plan, a pronouncement, or a wish — not a strategy.

The Strategy Test
Six diagnostic questions. If your strategy can't fail, it isn't one.

ISAP — Strategy Ideation, Not Implementation
A useful tool for what it is — and a dangerous one when mistaken for what it is not.

Operational Art
The cognitive bridge between strategic objectives and tactical action — across time, space, and operational periods.

Common Strategic Failures
Recurring patterns that mistake activity for strategy.

Theory of Action
The cause-and-effect logic that connects what to why.

THE CHAPTER'S CLAIM

A planning process that produces documentation without a coherent theory of action produces compliance — *not strategy.*

PARENT REFERENCE
OLFG Ch. 2, pages 59–116.

RELATED CHAPTERS
Ch. 3 (Red Teaming) ·
Ch. 7 (Contingency & Adaptation)

Four Things People Call Strategy

Four documents commonly mistaken for strategy. Each one does something — but only one connects what you do to why.

A CHECKLIST

"Here is everything we will do."

A list of tasks, often comprehensive, that describes activity without explaining how that activity produces effect.

What it lacks
A theory connecting actions to outcomes. Items get checked off, the strategic picture deteriorates anyway.

How to recognize
No one can articulate why a given task is on the list — only that it is.

A PLAN

"Here is the sequence we will follow."

A sequenced set of actions with timelines, resources, and identified dependencies. Useful — and necessary.

What it lacks
The reasoning behind the choices. A plan describes what to do. It does not explain why this and not that.

How to recognize
The plan survives even when conditions that justified it no longer hold.

A PRONOUNCEMENT

"We will achieve excellence in suppression."

A bold statement about priorities or aspirations, often delivered with confidence and a sense of direction.

What it lacks
Specificity. No defined end state, no named tradeoffs, no testable claim. Rhetoric substituting for commitment.

How to recognize
It cannot be falsified. Anything could count as success — or failure.

A STRATEGY

"This is how what we do produces what we need."

A coherent theory of action: ends, ways, means, and risk, tied together by explicit cause-and-effect logic.

What it requires
An end state. A theory of action. A resource commitment. An acknowledged tradeoff. All four, traceable.

How to recognize
It is specific enough to be wrong. It can be tested. It can be falsified.

If your strategy cannot be wrong, it is not a strategy. It is rhetoric.

TOOL · THE FOUR ELEMENTS

Ends · Ways · Means · Risk

THE LESSON
A strategy connects four elements. Missing any one means
you have a plan, a pronouncement, or a wish — not a strategy.

ENDS
The desired end state

In observable, measurable terms. Not 'contain the fire' — what does contained
look like, where, by when, with what acceptable cost. An end state that cannot
be achieved with the resources available is not strategic vision. It is fantasy.

WAYS
The theory of action

How the chosen approach will produce the desired outcome. The cause-and-effect
logic that connects what you do to what you achieve. The theory must be explicit,
not assumed. You must be able to articulate why you believe it will work.

MEANS
The resources available

Personnel, equipment, time, authority, political capital. If maximum available
does not exceed minimum required, the strategy must change. Scale it, delay it,
or redefine success. There is no third option.

RISK
What you will accept

Under what conditions the tradeoff becomes unacceptable. Risk that is implicitly
accepted cannot be monitored. Name what you are willing to lose, and name the
conditions that would tell you the bet is going wrong.

WHAT'S MISSING TELLS YOU WHAT YOU HAVE

Missing ends → a wish.   **Missing ways** → a plan.   **Missing means** → a fantasy.

Missing risk → exposure you cannot monitor.

Strategy connects all four. Anything less is something else.

THE TEST · BEFORE COMMITTING

Strategy Test

Six diagnostic questions. Run before approving direction.

THE LESSON

If a strategy cannot be wrong, it cannot be tested. If it cannot be tested, it is not a strategy. It is rhetoric.

1　**Can you state the theory of success in plain language?**

The cause-and-effect narrative that explains how actions lead to the end state.

ANSWER IT　　*— in your own words, out loud, to a peer who will push back.*

2　**Is the strategy specific enough to be wrong?**

If it cannot be falsified, it cannot be tested. Vagueness is the most common evasion.

ANSWER IT　　*— in your own words, out loud, to a peer who will push back.*

3　**If resources are cut by 30%, which objectives survive?**

Which are necessary versus desirable? A strategy that requires full resourcing is hope.

ANSWER IT　　*— in your own words, out loud, to a peer who will push back.*

4　**What are you choosing not to do?**

Strategy requires explicit choices about what to omit — and the cost of those omissions.

ANSWER IT　　*— in your own words, out loud, to a peer who will push back.*

5　**Compared to the best alternative, why is this one better?**

One sentence. If you cannot answer in one sentence, you have not considered the alternative.

ANSWER IT　　*— in your own words, out loud, to a peer who will push back.*

6　**Where does the logic depend on a leap rather than a link?**

Identify the weakest causal connection. That is where the strategy will break first.

ANSWER IT　　*— in your own words, out loud, to a peer who will push back.*

A strategy that fails any of these is not failed — it is unfinished.

TOOL · BOUNDARY OF SCOPE

ISAP

Strategy ideation — not strategy implementation.

THE LESSON

The Incident Strategic Alignment Process is a valuable tool for what it was designed to do. It is a dangerous tool when mistaken for what it was not.

WHAT ISAP DOES — AND DOES NOT — DO

WHAT ISAP IS	WHAT ISAP IS NOT
Strategy ideation.	**Strategy implementation.**
Initial goal-setting and exploratory discussion. High-level conceptualization of the incident and potential responses.	Detailed planning, resource allocation, operational sequencing, continuous monitoring, adaptive adjustment.
WHAT IT GENERATES	**WHAT IT DOES NOT GENERATE**
• Alignment between the IMT, the agency administrator, and stakeholders. • Initial strategic direction. • A shared starting picture. • Conditions for stakeholder engagement and dialogue.	• Measurable objectives. • Scenario-based contingencies. • Feedback loops for evaluation. • Discipline to adjust as conditions change.
USE ISAP TO	**DO NOT USE ISAP TO**
Open the strategic question. Generate alignment on direction. Surface assumptions early.	Close the strategic question. Substitute for ongoing strategic work. Declare a strategy "complete."

THE DANGER

Treating ISAP as if completing it means you have a strategy. You do not. You have the beginning of one. The work that *translates ideation into implementation has not yet begun.*

CONCEPT · THE BRIDGE

Operational Art

Translating strategy into action — across time and space.

THE LESSON

Operational art is the cognitive approach by which leaders translate strategic objectives into operational and tactical actions. It is the mechanism connecting ends to means.

THE QUESTION IT ANSWERS

Given this strategic objective, this set of resources, and this environment — how do I sequence and integrate tactical actions across time and space to produce strategic effect?

THREE LEVELS — AND THE BRIDGE BETWEEN THEM

STRATEGIC

Where objectives are defined. Ends, ways, means, risk.

OPERATIONAL — THE ART

Sequence. Integrate. Connect today's action to next week's effect.

The work done by OSCs, branch directors, and ICs when they connect daily operational plans to the strategic end state.

TACTICAL

Where actions are executed. Today's tasks, today's resources.

CAMPAIGN, NOT INDIVIDUAL BATTLES

Operational art requires leaders to think in terms of campaigns rather than individual operational periods.

- A single operational period is a battle.
- A sequence of periods, integrated to a progressive effect, is a campaign.

THE FAILURE MODE

Leaders who plan one operational period at a time without connecting those periods to a strategic arc are fighting a new war every day.

WATCH FOR · FOUR PATTERNS

Common Strategic Failures

Each of these failures has identifiable upstream causes.
Name them before they name you.

PREGNANT WITH THE PLAN

Resistance to information that contradicts the current plan. Sunk cost. Attribution of failure to external factors rather than to a strategy that no longer fits.

UPSTREAM CAUSE:

Identification with the plan as achievement rather than hypothesis.

ACTIVITY CONFUSED WITH PROGRESS

Tactical actions succeed but the strategic picture deteriorates. Outputs are measured; outcomes are not. The team is busy. The strategy is not advancing.

UPSTREAM CAUSE:

Measurement systems that reward what is countable, not what matters.

BOLD PRONOUNCEMENT AS STRATEGY

Vague language about priorities with no specificity about what will be done, with what, by when. Rhetoric substituting for commitment.

UPSTREAM CAUSE:

Cultural pressure to appear decisive without doing the work.

PLANNING BEYOND WHAT IS KNOWABLE

Detailed plans for operational periods that cannot be predicted. Cultural pressure to demonstrate foresight produces fiction — documented and circulated.

UPSTREAM CAUSE:

Confusing documentation of a plan with confidence in the outcome.

THE COMMON THREAD

All four failures share a structure: motion substituting for thought; documentation substituting for clarity; confidence *substituting for capability.*

TOOL · THREE-PART STRUCTURE

Theory of Action

The cause-and-effect logic that connects what to why.

THE LESSON

Strategy is a theory: a stated belief about how your chosen actions will produce the intended end state. Theories must be specific enough to be wrong.

THREE THINGS A THEORY OF ACTION MUST CONNECT

01 END STATE

ASK YOURSELF

What specific, observable condition do you intend to produce?

REQUIRED ELEMENTS

• A describable state, not a general aspiration.

• Realistic given the resources available.

• A standard against which progress is measured.

Without this, you have a wish, not a strategy.

02 THEORY OF ACTION

ASK YOURSELF

How will the chosen approach produce that end state?

REQUIRED ELEMENTS

• Explicit, not assumed.

• Based on stated assumptions about how the system will respond.

• Specific enough that you would recognize it failing.

Without this, you have a plan, not a strategy.

03 MEASURABLE COMMITMENT

ASK YOURSELF

What are you committing to do — and not do — and how will you know if it's working?

REQUIRED ELEMENTS

• Concrete actions with resources and timelines.

• Decision points where you reassess.

• Indicators that the theory is — or is not — holding.

Without this, you have a pronouncement.

THE TEST OF THE THEORY

A strategy must be specific enough to be wrong.
If it cannot fail, it is not a strategy. It is rhetoric.

CHAPTER CLOSE · DIAGNOSTIC PATTERNS

Watch For

When strategic thinking is failing in your operation.

Strategic failure rarely announces itself with a single bad decision. It accumulates through patterns. These are the signals that the strategic foundation is failing — not the plan.

PATTERN · DRIFTING END STATE

The strategy keeps changing — but no one named the change.

- Today's objectives don't match yesterday's. No one decided to revise.
- The end state is described differently by different leaders.
- Daily plans assume different futures.
- "What does done look like?" produces a long pause.

Diagnosis: No defined end state, or end state changing silently.

First test: Ask three division supervisors to describe success.

PATTERN · ACTIVITY WITHOUT TRACE

Tactical actions cannot be traced back to strategic ends.

- Outputs aggregate but the strategic picture does not change.
- Successful tactical actions don't visibly advance the end state.
- "Why are we doing this?" produces tactical answers, not strategic ones.
- Resources flow to what feels urgent, not to what advances strategy.

Diagnosis: Theory of action absent or untestable.

First test: Trace one day's outputs to the strategic end state.

PATTERN · UNFALSIFIABLE STRATEGY

The strategy cannot be tested — and therefore cannot be wrong.

- Anything could count as success — or as failure.
- The team cannot articulate what would change the strategy.
- Bad news is reframed as a different success.
- The strategy has not changed despite material condition changes.

Diagnosis: Strategy is rhetoric — pronouncement disguised as plan.

First test: Apply the Strategy Test (p. 42). All six questions.

SEE ALSO

Strategic failures cascade into Ch. 3 (Red Teaming — where they should have been challenged) and Ch. 7 (Contingency & Adaptation — where they should have been revised). Section IV maps the cascades.

TOOL · MAKE THE CAUSAL LOGIC EXPLICIT

Theory of Action

Ways is the element that fails most often, and most quietly. The failure is not that the theory is wrong — it is never written down.

THE LESSON

A theory of action is the causal chain connecting what you do to what you achieve — stated as logic, not a sequence of events.

THE STRUCTURE OF A THEORY OF ACTION

IF (X)	THEN (Y)	BECAUSE (Z)
We do the action	*We expect the outcome*	*The mechanism makes it so*
the task	the condition	the reason to believe

The middle term (Z) is what most plans omit. The discipline is to write it down.

FOUR ELEMENTS MAKE IT OPERATIONAL

01   **THE CHAIN**
Tasks → mechanisms → intermediate objective → end state. Each link concrete enough that another could evaluate it.

02   **THE ASSUMPTIONS**
What must be true for each link to hold — the load-bearing ones whose failure would invalidate the chain.

03   **THE INDICATORS**
What you would observe if an assumption were starting to fail. The trip-wires that connect theory to the field.

04   **REVISION TRIGGERS**
What you would do — pre-decided — if an indicator surfaced. The triggers are what make the theory adaptive.

A plan names X and Y — it can be executed but not evaluated. A theory of action names X, Y, and Z — it can be evaluated, monitored, and revised.

TOOL · TWO QUESTIONS, SIMILAR WORDS, DIFFERENT ANSWERS

Performance vs. Effectiveness

Reporting performance without effectiveness is how a strategy fails invisibly — while every status board reports the plan on track.

MEASURE OF PERFORMANCE **Did we do what we said we would do?**	MEASURE OF EFFECTIVENESS **Did doing it produce the condition intended?**
WHAT IT IS	
A count of activity — discrete, attributable units of work the team performed.	A description of a condition — a state of the world the team is trying to bring about.
EXAMPLES	
Miles of line constructed. Structures wrapped. Drops delivered. Briefings conducted.	The line is holding. Structures stand after the wind. Spread slowed. DIVS back-brief the intent.
WHAT IT VERIFIES	
That the plan was executed. Indispensable for daily reporting.	That execution produced the intended effect. Tells you whether the strategy is working.
WHAT ITS ABSENCE PRODUCES	
A strategy nobody can verify is being executed. Rare — this is the cultural default.	A strategy that fails invisibly while reports show the plan on track. The recurring failure.

THE DISCIPLINE
Ask both, separately, every time. The two questions look similar enough that they can be answered with the same words. They are different questions.

A theory of action with only performance measures cannot be tested.
A theory with effectiveness measures can.

TOOL · THE LINE OF EFFORT DIAGNOSTIC

Lines of Effort

Tasks can be grouped five ways. Each is valid for its own purpose.
Only one of them produces a line of effort.

THE LESSON
A line of effort is a theory of action at strand level: tasks grouped by
the condition they establish, not by who, when, where, or what does them.

GROUPING PRINCIPLE	QUESTION IT ANSWERS	PRODUCES	LOE?
Function *Operations, Logistics, Plans.*	Who does them?	Sections	NO
Time *Day-shift, night-shift, opening.*	When do they happen?	Phases	NO
Geography *Division Charlie, Division Bravo.*	Where do they happen?	Divisions / Branches	NO
Resource *The Type 1 crew, the aviation block.*	What does them?	Resource orders	NO
Purpose *Community protection, welfare.*	**What condition do they establish?**	**Lines of Effort**	✓ YES

THE DIAGNOSTIC
What condition is this task intended to establish,
and what other tasks share that condition?

The diagnostic is the condition, not the appearance. The first question
groups by what tasks have in common. Only the second produces a line of effort.

TOOL · FOUR PHASES, FOUR COGNITIVE DEMANDS

The Division Assignment Arc

A DIVS joins mid-assignment, holds it for a few periods, and hands it off while the incident still runs. The arc is short and bounded.

THE LESSON
Each phase has a dominant cognitive demand, a characteristic failure mode, and a specific relationship to the lines of effort the DIVS feeds.

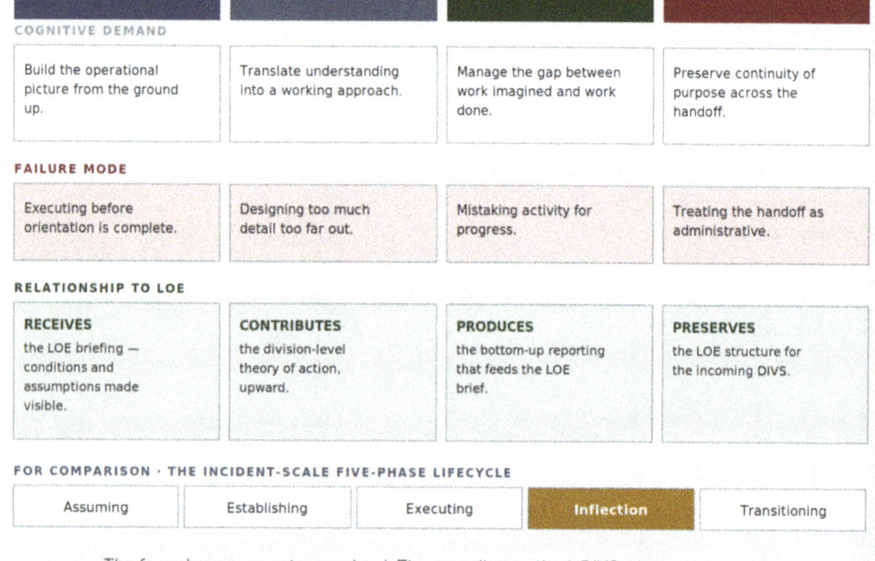

The four phases are not procedural. They are diagnostic. A DIVS who can recognize which phase they are in operates with a coherence tactical instinct cannot produce.

The LOE Assessment Brief

Four elements, none optional. The brief tests the theory of action, not the activity count. Two to three minutes per line of effort.

THE LESSON
The inputs are not a separate channel — they come from the post-ops SAPPER debrief the daily rhythm already produces, filtered through the line of effort's theory of action.

FOUR ELEMENTS, NONE OPTIONAL

01 **PERFORMANCE**   · *what we did*
Are we executing the tasks we said we would? Brief enough to confirm the work is happening. If performance is the only thing reported, the brief is failing.

02 **EFFECTIVENESS**   · *what is changing*
Is the condition this line of effort exists to establish actually moving? Cite the measure of effectiveness. Activity without effect is what this element catches.

03 **ASSUMPTIONS**   · *what the theory depends on*
Status of the assumptions: still holding, under stress, or broken. An assumption that quietly shifted to broken is how a line of effort dies unnoticed.

04 **ADAPTATION TRIGGERS**   · *what would change the approach*
Observations that should change the line of effort itself — not adjustments within it. A trigger reached and not surfaced is the worst outcome of the brief.

THE DIAGNOSTIC
A brief of only performance is a status report, not an assessment. A brief that never names a trigger has stopped looking for one.

The line of effort is a hypothesis. The brief is how the hypothesis is tested.

CHAPTER 3 OF 11

Red Teaming

Critical thinking and decision challenge.

Stress-test plans before reality does — with the structure
and facilitation discipline to make dissent safe and useful.

*Red teaming is not about finding fault. It is about finding
the truth before the truth finds you.*

IN THIS CHAPTER

Cognitive Failure Modes
Groupthink, fallacies, biases — the predictable ways
teams fool themselves under operational pressure.

Six Tool Categories
When to reach for each. Not every tool is right for every
moment — match the tool to the cognitive failure.

Key Assumptions Check — Every Time
The single most consequential tool in this chapter. Surface
the unstated. Monitor what would tell you it is wrong.

Premortem Analysis
Assume the plan has failed. Now explain why.

Designated Challenger
The structural intervention that interrupts advocacy drift.

Six Strategic Questions · Four Ways of Seeing
Stress-test the plan from outside the planning tent.

Inquiry vs. Advocacy
The shift that degrades decision quality — and the
facilitation discipline that pushes back.

THE CHAPTER'S CLAIM

If your team has never told you your plan has a problem,
the most likely explanation is not that your plans are
flawless. It is that challenge is not welcome.

PARENT REFERENCE
OLFG Ch. 3, pages 117–148.

RELATED CHAPTERS
Ch. 4 (Decision Quality) ·
Ch. 7 (Contingency & Adaptation)

WHAT RED TEAMING INTERRUPTS

Cognitive Failure Modes

THE LESSON

Teams under operational pressure fail in predictable ways. Red teaming exists to interrupt the failures before they become the after-action.

GROUPTHINK

The cohesive team converges on a single view and treats disagreement as disloyalty. Bad ideas survive because challenging them feels like betrayal.

Antidote: structured dissent.
Designated challenger. Think-Write-Share.

CONFIRMATION BIAS

The team weighs evidence that supports the current plan more heavily than evidence that contradicts it. Disconfirming data is explained away rather than examined.

Antidote: name the assumptions.
Key Assumptions Check. Premortem.

ANCHORING

The first number, first option, or first assessment becomes the reference point — and subsequent thinking adjusts from there instead of starting fresh.

Antidote: independent first pass.
Think-Write-Share. Separate option generation.

SUNK COST FALLACY

Continuing a course because of what has already been invested, rather than because the future returns justify continuing. Pregnant with the plan.

Antidote: fresh-eyes reframe.
Premortem. Strategy Test (Ch. 2 p. 42).

AVAILABILITY HEURISTIC

Recent or vivid events feel more probable than they are. The last fire's behavior becomes the model for this one — even when the conditions are different.

Antidote: base-rate reasoning.
Compare to historical patterns, not memory.

ESCALATION OF COMMITMENT

The deeper the team is in, the harder it becomes to pull back — even when the evidence says pulling back is correct. Doubling down on a failing strategy.

Antidote: pre-committed triggers.
Decide in advance what would change the call.

Red teaming tools are not a fix. They are a discipline.
The failure modes return whenever the discipline lapses.

TOOL · MATCHING TOOL TO MOMENT

Six Tool Categories

Different cognitive failures need different tools. The skill is matching the tool to the moment — not running every tool every time.

01   COLLABORATIVE THINKING & DIALOGUE

Surface diverse perspectives. Generate ideas before evaluating them.

Use when: Multiple perspectives needed. Loudest voice isn't best informed.

TOOLS Think-Write-Share · 1-2-4-Whole Group · Fishbowl · Circle of Voices

02   PROBLEM FRAMING & SHARED UNDERSTANDING

Clarify, reframe, or deepen the team's understanding of an issue.

Use when: Team is solving the wrong problem. Stakeholders have different pictures.

TOOLS Problem Restatement · 5 Whys · Frame Audit · Outside-In Thinking

03   ASSUMPTION TESTING & RED TEAMING

Surface hidden assumptions, test plan logic, explore competing views.

Use when: Before committing to a course of action. When consequences are severe.

TOOLS Key Assumptions Check · Premortem · Analysis of Competing Hypotheses

04   STRATEGIC COMMUNICATION & NARRATIVE

Improve how ideas are expressed, perceived, and agreed upon.

Use when: Briefings produce different conclusions. Intended message not landing.

TOOLS SEEI · 6 Words · 4 Ways of Seeing · My 15%

05   DECISION SUPPORT & OPTIONS DEVELOPMENT

Identify alternatives. Surface creative options. Examine trade-offs.

Use when: One COA on the table. Trade-offs not yet examined.

TOOLS Stakeholder Mapping · BATNA · 5 Will Get You 25 · Outside-In Thinking

06   COACHING & PEER CONSULTATION

Peer-to-peer insight, reflective challenge, structured mentoring.

Use when: A leader works through a problem with structured input from peers.

TOOLS Troika Consulting · Think-Write-Share · Yes-And

TOOL · THE EVERY-TIME TOOL

Key Assumptions Check

THE LESSON

Every plan rests on assumptions. Most are never stated, let alone tested. Assumptions you don't surface can't be monitored. Assumptions you don't monitor will fail without warning.

THE PROCESS — FIVE STEPS   ~60 MIN

1 · STATE

State the current plan, decision, or analytic line clearly enough that everyone in the room shares the same picture of what is being tested.

2 · LIST

List every premise that must be true for the plan to succeed — both stated and unstated. Surface the assumptions no one wrote down.

3 · INTERROGATE

For each assumption, ask: Why must this be true? Is it evidence, preconception, or historical analogy? Is it valid under all conditions? When would it fail?

4 · REFINE

Reduce the list to only those assumptions that are truly critical — the ones the plan cannot survive without.

5 · INSTRUMENT

For each critical assumption, identify what observable information would tell you it is no longer valid. These are your trip-wires.

THE PAYOFF — TRIP-WIRES

Every critical assumption gets three components.

ASSUMPTION

What you believe must be true for the plan to work.

> **INDICATOR**

What you would observe if the assumption were failing.

> **RESPONSE**

What you will do — pre-decided — when the indicator appears.

If you do nothing else from this chapter, do this.

TOOL · PROSPECTIVE HINDSIGHT

Premortem Analysis

THE LESSON

"What could go wrong?" produces defense of the plan.
"The plan has failed — tell me why" produces explanation
of the failure. The shift surfaces what defense never will.

THE FRAMING — SAY IT EXACTLY

**"It is six weeks from now. The plan has failed.
Tell me the story of how it failed."**

Narrative form. Past tense. Specific.

THE PROCESS

STEP 1 · INDIVIDUAL REFLECTION (10 MIN)

Each person silently writes the story of the failure. Specific causes. Specific
consequences. No filtering. The point is to generate, not yet to evaluate.

Independent writing prevents the loudest voice from anchoring the discussion.

STEP 2 · ROUND-ROBIN SHARING (20 MIN)

Each person reads one cause. Continue around the table until all are surfaced.
No debate yet. Capture every failure mode.

The discipline is generation, not refinement. Refinement comes next.

STEP 3 · MITIGATE OR TRIGGER (30 MIN)

For each surfaced failure: either mitigate (build it into the plan) or trigger
(define the condition under which a contingency activates).

A surfaced failure with no response is the worst outcome — you know and you didn't act.

TWO VALID OUTPUTS

MITIGATION

A change to the plan that addresses the surfaced failure. Built in
before execution begins.

TRIGGER

A condition that activates a contingency. Pre-decided.

Better the failure surface in the planning room than on the ground.

TOOL · STRUCTURAL INTERVENTION

Designated Challenger

THE LESSON

Once a preferred COA emerges, the conversation shifts from inquiry to advocacy. The challenger is the structural intervention that pushes it back.

HOW IT WORKS

Before the COA is finalized, one person is assigned the explicit role of arguing against it — making the strongest possible case it will not work.

The challenger is not voicing personal disagreement. They are executing a role. Other participants know this, which lowers the social cost of the challenge and frees the challenger to surface concerns they would self-censor.

WHO GETS THE ROLE

NOT
The most cynical voice — the team will discount predictable contrarianism. The substance gets lost in the framing.

ONE OF
The most credible and creative thinkers — someone whose judgment the group respects, and whose challenge cannot be dismissed as posturing.

ROTATED
Across decisions when possible — builds the discipline across the team.

THREE VALID OUTPUTS

MODIFICATIONS
Specific changes that address the surfaced objections.

MITIGATIONS
Measures that reduce the consequence of identified vulnerabilities.

TRIGGERS
Conditions under which a pre-planned fallback engages.

If the plan survives a serious effort to defeat it, the team executes with greater confidence. If it doesn't, the failure surfaces in the planning room — not on the ground.

TOOLS · TWO COMPLEMENTARY LENSES

Six Strategic Questions
& Four Ways of Seeing

Six questions test the plan from inside the planning tent.
Four perspectives test it from outside. Use together.

SIX STRATEGIC QUESTIONS — RUN AT EVERY APPROVAL POINT

1. What problem are we solving — and what problem are we accidentally solving instead?

2. What does success look like in observable, measurable terms — and by when?

3. What are we choosing not to do — and what does that choice cost us if we are wrong?

4. Compared to the best alternative strategy, why is this one better? (One sentence.)

5. Where does the logic of this strategy depend on a leap rather than a link?

6. What single point of failure could collapse this strategy — and what is our response if it does?

Use at: strategy approval, objective changes, operational period transitions, when conditions materially change.

Skip any one and the corresponding category remains untested.

FOUR WAYS OF SEEING — RUN BEFORE COMMITTING

HOW WE SEE OURSELVES

The plan as we have written it. Our intent, our capabilities, our reasoning. The view from inside the planning tent.

HOW WE SEE THEM

Our assessment of conditions, the fire, the stakeholders, the agency administrator, the public. The view we have constructed of everyone else.

HOW THEY SEE US

How the agency administrator, the public, the cooperators see our team. Often surprisingly different from the view in the planning tent.

HOW THEY SEE THEMSELVES

How the other actors understand their own situation, priorities, constraints, and intent. The view from inside their tent.

The gap between any two views is information.

Inquiry vs. Advocacy

THE LESSON

Once a preferred COA emerges, the room shifts from "what should we do?" to "how do we justify what we have already started doing?" The shift is rarely deliberate.

TWO MODES — WHICH ONE IS THE ROOM IN?

INQUIRY MODE *"What should we do?"*	ADVOCACY MODE *"How do we justify this?"*
THE DISPOSITION Open evaluation of options. Trade-offs surfaced and weighed. Best ideas can come from anyone. Disagreement is information.	**THE DISPOSITION** Defending the forming option. Trade-offs minimized or hidden. Senior view becomes the answer. Disagreement is friction.
VERBS YOU HEAR "Consider..." "What if..." "Help me understand..." "Compared to..."	**VERBS YOU HEAR** "We need to..." "The plan is..." "As I said before..." "Let's not relitigate..."
PROTECTS Decision quality. *Cost: time. Discomfort.*	**PROTECTS** Momentum. *Cost: decision quality.*

THE FACILITATOR'S DIAGNOSTIC

Listen for the verbs in the room. They tell you which mode is dominant. When you hear advocacy verbs at a moment that needs inquiry, intervene.

"Before we lock this, what would change our minds?"
A single question can push the room back toward inquiry.

THE STRUCTURAL REPAIR

The Designated Challenger (p. 53) is the repair when *facilitation alone cannot resist the drift.*

Watch For

When the technique is sound but execution breaks.

Red teaming tools fail when facilitation fails. The technique is sound; the execution is what breaks. These are the failure patterns to watch — and the immediate repairs for each.

PATTERN · DOMINANT VOICES

The senior person speaks first. The group converges on their view.

- Air time skews to the most senior or most assertive.
- Discussion never widens beyond the first option presented.
- Quiet members are silent — or agree without elaboration.

Repair: Think-Write-Share. Independent reflection before discussion.

PATTERN · LEADING QUESTIONS

The facilitator is advocating, not inquiring.

- Questions assume the answer ("Don't we all agree...?").
- Disconfirming responses get reframed as agreement.
- Closed yes/no questions where open questions belong.

Repair: Watch your verbs. Replace "Don't you agree" with "What concerns you?"

PATTERN · FAILURE TO CLOSE

The session was a conversation, not a working session.

- Issues surfaced but no decisions recorded.
- No owners assigned to identified vulnerabilities.
- No triggers set. No contingencies built.

Repair: Every surfaced issue → mitigation or trigger, with named owner.

PATTERN · FALSE CONSENSUS

Silence is read as agreement. It is not the same as alignment.

- Heads nodding around the table without verbal commitment.
- The most affected member has not spoken.
- Concerns surface privately after the meeting ends.

Repair: Ask each person directly. By name. Out loud.

SEE ALSO

Facilitation failures cascade into Ch. 4 (Decision Quality — where they degrade the decision) and Ch. 8 (AAR & Learning — where they prevent the lesson from being learned).

CHAPTER 4 OF 11

Decision Quality

Process you control. Outcomes you don't.

Separate the quality of a decision from the quality of its
outcome. Good decisions can produce bad outcomes through
factors beyond your control. Bad decisions can produce
good outcomes through luck.

Confuse the two and you learn the wrong lessons.

IN THIS CHAPTER

Decision Quality vs. Decision Outcome
A 2×2 matrix. Four possible relationships. Two that look
like one — and the cost of mistaking them.

The Six-Question Framework
Evaluate the process, not the result. Use before commitment
as a check. Use after as a frame for the AAR.

What Degrades Decision Quality
Recurring patterns inside the process — where the failure
happens before the moment of choice.

Decision Inertia
The failure mode that looks like prudence — gathering more
information instead of making the call.

Least-Worst Decisions
When every option has cost. Naming the tradeoff explicitly.

THE CHAPTER'S CLAIM

Process is what you control.
Outcome is what you get.

PARENT REFERENCE
OLFG Ch. 4, pages 149–224.

RELATED CHAPTERS
Ch. 3 (Red Teaming) ·
Ch. 8 (AAR & Learning)

THE FOUNDATIONAL DISTINCTION

Decision Quality
vs. Outcome Quality

THE LESSON

Good decisions can produce bad outcomes through factors beyond your control. Bad decisions can produce good outcomes through luck. Evaluating on outcome alone reinforces both.

FOUR POSSIBLE RELATIONSHIPS

OUTCOME

GOOD

WARRANTED LOSS	DESERVED SUCCESS
Poor process · Good outcome	*Sound process · Good outcome*
"Lucky."	**"What you're aiming for."**
The team is reinforced for a process that will eventually fail.	Process produced the outcome.
MOST DANGEROUS	**REPLICABLE**
PROCESS FAILURE	BAD BREAK
Poor process · Poor outcome	*Sound process · Poor outcome*
"Predictable."	**"The wind shifted."**
The system produced exactly what the process supports.	The radio failed. Conditions overrode the decision.
FIX THE PROCESS	**LEARN THE ENVIRONMENT**

POOR

← POOR   DECISION QUALITY (PROCESS)   SOUND

THE DISCIPLINE

Scrutinize good outcomes as hard as bad ones.
The most dangerous decisions in your career are the bad ones that worked out.

TOOL · THE DIAGNOSTIC

Six-Question Framework

THE LESSON

Evaluate decisions on process, not outcome. Use during the decision to build discipline. Use after to evaluate quality.

1 PROBLEM

Was the right problem identified — or were we solving the wrong one?

Unclear problems cascade into every subsequent step. Each leader fills the vacuum with their own interpretation.

2 ASSUMPTIONS

Were the assumptions tested before commitment?

Untested assumptions become hidden vulnerabilities. KAC is the discipline; this question is the audit.

3 ALTERNATIVES

Were alternatives genuinely evaluated, or was one option ratified?

If only one COA was considered, the decision process was incomplete — regardless of the outcome.

4 INFORMATION

Was decision-relevant information sought — or just what was in the room?

What was in the room is rarely complete. What was sought is what you trusted enough to test.

5 REASONING

Was the reasoning communicated in a way the team could verify and challenge?

Reasoning you cannot articulate is reasoning your team cannot test — or correct when conditions change.

6 REVISABILITY

Was the decision revisable when conditions changed — or did it become fixed?

A decision that cannot be revised is a commitment, not a choice.

WHEN TO USE

During the decision — build process discipline. Answer each before commitment.
After the decision — evaluate quality independent of how the outcome turned out.

FAILURE PATTERNS INSIDE THE PROCESS

What Degrades
Decision Quality

*A decision that produced a bad outcome rarely failed at the
moment of choice. It failed earlier — in framing, in alternatives,
in information, or in how it was communicated.*

ANALYTICAL COMPLETENESS — THE ILLUSION

More analysis feels like more rigor. It often is not. Past a certain
threshold, additional analysis produces diminishing returns — and
increasing confidence that is not warranted by the underlying evidence.

WATCH FOR

*Data volume substituting for data quality. Confidence rising with
effort spent, regardless of what the effort actually surfaced.*

AUTHORITY OF EXPERIENCE WITHOUT SCRUTINY

Experienced leaders make confident calls in conditions that look like
what they have seen before. When the conditions are actually different,
experience accelerates the wrong decision — and the team defers.

WATCH FOR

*"We have seen this before" without testing whether what follows from
that comparison still holds under current conditions.*

TREATING PROXIES AS THE REAL THING

Metrics, models, and indicators are stand-ins for the underlying reality.
Substituting them for the reality itself produces decisions optimized
for the proxy — not for what the proxy was meant to represent.

WATCH FOR

*Containment percentage discussed as if it were operational control.
Engagement scores discussed as if they were team health.*

CONFUSING RISK REDUCTION WITH CONSEQUENCE MITIGATION

Risk reduction lowers the probability. Consequence mitigation reduces
the cost if the bad event occurs. These are different decisions with
different tradeoffs — and they often get conflated.

WATCH FOR

*A single mitigation claimed to do both. They almost never
do both well.*

FAILURE MODE THAT LOOKS LIKE PRUDENCE

Decision Inertia

THE LESSON

A failure mode that does not look like failure. It looks like prudence — gathering more information, consulting more people. The cognitive activity is real. The action is not.

FIVE CONDITIONS THAT INCREASE INERTIA

- **Ambiguous information** about the decision problem.

- **High-stakes consequences** for being wrong.

- **Competing values** — any choice betrays something the leader holds important.

- **Limited domain experience** in the exact conditions presenting.

- **Individual disposition** toward indecision.

Recognize the conditions. Inertia under these conditions is predictable, not personal — and therefore can be planned for.

THREE PRACTICES TO REDUCE IT

SET DEADLINES

"I will decide by 1400 with the information I have at 1400."
Forces the question: is the cost of waiting greater than the cost of deciding?

NAME WHAT WOULD CHANGE THE CALL

Articulate what additional information would actually change the decision.
If you cannot name it, gathering more is delay — not analysis.

DIAGNOSE THE URGE TO CONSULT

Treat the urge to consult one more person as a diagnostic — sometimes information gap, more often accountability spreading.

Inertia is decision-making by default.
The environment decides — and the leader bears the consequence.

WHEN EVERY OPTION HAS COST

Least-Worst Decisions

THE LESSON

When every option produces significant negative consequences,
the question is not which is good — it is which is least bad.
The skill is intellectual; the difficulty is emotional.

DO THIS

NAME THE TRADEOFF EXPLICITLY

What value is being subordinated to which other value, and why.
Implicit tradeoffs become surprise costs. Surprise costs break trust.

DOCUMENT THE REASONING BEFORE THE OUTCOME

Decision quality cannot be evaluated retroactively. Reasoning written
after the outcome is reasoning shaped by the outcome.

COMMUNICATE THE TRADEOFF

To those who will execute and to those affected. Surprise produces
broken trust — which outlasts the decision.

TWO FAILURE MODES

FREEZING

Making no decision at all. The environment decides instead.
*The cost of inaction is rarely zero — and is usually distributed to people
who did not choose to bear it.*

CHOOSING WHAT LOOKS BETTER BUT IS NOT ACHIEVABLE

Committing because the alternative is admitting the limit. Worse than
freezing — you have committed resources to a path you cannot complete.
The least-worst real option is better than the best fantasy option.

CALIBRATE THE LANGUAGE

The environment is uncertain. Your words should reflect that.
*False confidence in a least-worst decision degrades trust faster
than the bad outcome itself.*

Watch For

When decision quality is degrading in your operation.

*Process failures rarely announce themselves. They show up
in the language of the planning tent, in what gets discussed,
and in what gets ratified without examination.*

PATTERN · OUTCOME REASONING

Past decisions are judged on what happened, not on how they were made.

- Good outcomes are credited; bad outcomes are blamed.
- The leader who got lucky is celebrated; the leader who got unlucky is questioned.
- Process discussions are skipped — "it worked, didn't it?"
- AARs focus on what happened, not how decisions were reached.

Diagnosis: Outcome reasoning. The most dangerous failure mode.
Repair: Run the Six Questions (p. 59) on outcomes the team called "good."

PATTERN · ANALYTICAL STALL

The team is busy analyzing. No one is deciding.

- The same information has been reviewed multiple times.
- The list of "things we still need" keeps growing, not shrinking.
- Decision deadlines slip without anyone naming them.
- The team consults "one more person" repeatedly.

Diagnosis: Decision inertia. The environment is deciding for you.
Repair: Set a deadline. Name what would change the call. Decide.

PATTERN · RATIFIED PREFERENCE

The decision was reached before the meeting started.

- Only one option was seriously developed.
- Alternatives were named briefly, then dismissed.
- The leader's preference was known early — and not contested.
- Discussion focused on execution details, not the choice itself.

Diagnosis: Advocacy disguised as inquiry. See Ch. 3 (p. 55).
Repair: Assign a Designated Challenger before the next decision.

SEE ALSO

Decision quality failures cascade into Ch. 5 (Communication — where
they spread) and Ch. 8 (AAR & Learning — where they should be caught).
Section IV maps the diagnostic cascades.

DISCIPLINE · PRESERVE DECISION SPACE UNTIL THE SITUATION RESOLVES

Holding Multiple Possibilities

What to do when the options are not yet distinguishable — when committing early would foreclose options that may be the right ones.

THE LESSON

Hold the options open until the situation resolves the choice — rather than collapsing the set early to relieve the discomfort of unresolved deliberation or to satisfy the pressure that rewards visible decisiveness.

THE HARD PROBLEM

From the outside it looks identical to decision inertia. Same observable behavior — not yet committed. The internal state is what differs.

THE DIAGNOSTIC · TWO QUESTIONS

1. What information would distinguish the options?

2. When is that information expected to arrive?

WHAT THE ANSWERS TELL YOU

CAN ANSWER BOTH
Holding possibilities productively. The waiting is purposeful.

CAN ANSWER NEITHER
Decision inertia — regardless of how the deliberation looks.

FIRST BUT NOT SECOND
Neither discipline applies. Least-worst decision-making applies instead.

WHEN THE DISCIPLINE ENDS
Commit the moment the information arrives. Or commit on the best information available when the window is closing. To wait past either point is inertia — the discipline times the commitment, it does not avoid it.

Inertia is failing to commit when commitment is required. Holding possibilities is not committing when commitment is not yet required. Mirror images of one capacity.

FAILURE MODE · THE REJECTED ALTERNATIVE IN A NEW FRAME

Variation Without Mitigation

*A team rejects A on structural risk, develops B as a different option,
and approves B without testing whether what disqualified A applies.*

THE LESSON

When a structural condition disqualifies an alternative, that condition
becomes the test every subsequent alternative must clear. Until it is
addressed or explicitly accepted, every variation inherits it.

WHY THE PATTERN FORMS

SENSE OF COMPLETED WORK	FRAMED AS A NEW OPTION
Rejecting A feels like risk analysis done. But the finding was condition-level, not option-level — and the condition-level finding is the one that carries forward.	Calling B "a different option" invites the question does this meet our criteria? — not the question that matters: does this address what disqualified A?

THE QUESTION · ASK IT FIRST

*Before we evaluate this option on its own merits — what were the
conditions that disqualified the prior option, and does this one
address them?*

THE QUESTION PRODUCES THREE OUTCOMES

ADDRESSES THEM	DOES NOT	WHAT IS NOT LEGITIMATE
Proceed. Evaluate the option on its own characteristics.	Find another option, accept the risk explicitly, or change the end state.	Proceeding as if the new option were free of the disqualifying condition.

*The cost avoided: a line built under conditions already judged un-mitigable.
The cost incurred: thirty seconds that re-anchored the analysis. The trade is not close.*

TOOL · ALLOCATE AGAINST THE RIGHT PROBLEM AT THE RIGHT TEMPO

Phasing, Alignment & Fit

*A concern surfaces. The default is to convert it into an allocation —
which feels like action and is rewarded as decisiveness.*

THE LESSON

Three failures hide inside that move: phasing is skipped, the alignment
test is not run, capability-problem fit is not tested. The result may
address the surface concern, the actual problem, or neither.

THREE SEQUENTIAL MOVES · ABOUT TWO MINUTES TOGETHER

01

PHASING ANALYSIS

Name the temporal decision space. How much time is actually available to
allocate well — distinguished from how much the felt urgency implies?

Output: an explicit priority order the whole system runs on.

02

STRATEGIC ALIGNMENT TEST

A resource request is rarely about capability. Test whether the crews
already in the area understand the strategy before adding more.

Tactical circling is the diagnostic for strategic misalignment.

03

CAPABILITY-PROBLEM FIT

Name the actual problem the concern points to. Specify the capability it
requires. Test whether the available resource brings that capability.

Fits, fails to fit, or fits partially — do not plug a resource in because it is available.

*The three moves take roughly two minutes together. The cost of skipping them
is whatever the misallocation turns out to cost — rarely two minutes, often substantial.*

TOOL · WHY THE DISCIPLINE PAYS ABOVE THE INCIDENT

The Cascade of Benefit

Phasing discipline at the incident does not stay there. The system propagates whatever the incident produces upward.

THE LESSON

When the incident produces discipline, the discipline propagates as compounding benefit at every level above it — benefits the leader who installed it does not see directly, but that operate continuously.

THE DISCIPLINE PROPAGATES UPWARD

BEYOND THE ASSIGNMENT
Institutional reputation. The team carries demonstrated credibility into the next assignment.

AGENCY ADMINISTRATORS
The IC's brief is confirmed by their own sources. Trust becomes operational latitude.

SYSTEM-WIDE REPORTING
The ICS-209 matches reality. It becomes trusted source material, not a document to cross-check.

REGIONAL LEVEL
Resource requests carry coherent rationale. The Duty Officer reads them with default trust.

SUPPORTING SECTIONS
Logistics, Planning, Finance, Safety calibrate to the priority order without inferring it.

THE INCIDENT
Clear phasing produces coherent tactical execution. Divisions operate against explicit priorities.

THE BENEFIT IS INVISIBLE

The benefits show up as the absence of friction at the upper levels — not as visible rewards. The leader installs the discipline on a calculation that its cost is justified by benefits they will not see directly.

The disciplines do not produce dramatic moments.
They produce the absence of dramatic moments, at every level above.

TOOL · INSTALL THE DISCIPLINE BEFORE IT IS REQUIRED

Abundance & Atrophy

The discipline is hardest to install in the conditions where it is easiest to practice.

THE LESSON

The atrophy happens during abundance — in conditions where the cost of atrophy is invisible because the abundance is covering for it. Then scarcity arrives and the discipline becomes structurally necessary.

THE SAME DISCIPLINE, TWO CONDITIONS

ABUNDANCE early season · resources available	SCARCITY late season · PL 4-5 · acute competition
• The discipline does not feel necessary.	• Every allocation has visible cost.
• Imprecise allocation is absorbed by the abundance.	• Every request competes across incidents.
• Cultural pressure to practice is low.	• The conditions force the discipline.
• The habit never gets built. Atrophy is invisible.	• Those who never practiced must now — at far higher cost.

THE CORRECTIVE

Install the discipline when it is not yet required. The practice built in low-stakes conditions is what becomes available when scarcity arrives. The leader who waits for conditions to force it has waited too long.

THE DIAGNOSTIC

Not: has the operator been doing this a long time? But: did the conditions they developed their habits under require the discipline — or permit substituting abundance for it?

The discipline built in low-stakes conditions is what carries the team through the high-stakes conditions where the discipline is required.

FAILURE MODE · GAPS THE PERSON CANNOT SEE

Identity Defense

The feedback does not land — not because the operator rejected it, but because they do not experience it as accurate.

THE LESSON

Identity-protective cognition processes information that threatens a valued identity differently. The protective work is done before conscious processing begins. It is not laziness, resistance, or arrogance.

THE MECHANISM

When information threatens standing in a group central to identity, the cognitive system rejects or reframes it before it reaches deliberative evaluation. The person does not decide to reject the feedback. They experience it as untrue.

Greater analytical ability builds a better defense, not a more objective evaluation.

FOUR AMPLIFIERS IN THE FIRE SERVICE

IDENTITY ANCHOR STRENGTH

Crew, IMT, tenure, lineage are load-bearing for self-concept, not just credentials.

COST OF ADMITTED LIMITATION

Admitting a gap in front of peers carries real, persistent social cost.

IDENTITY-ANCHORING PROXIES

Patches, positions, callsigns get treated as the capability, not a shortcut for it.

OPERATIONAL TEMPO

The pace rarely permits the slow evaluation that would surface the gap.

THE DISCIPLINE

Asking someone to be open does not reach the protective layer. Work around the mechanism through structure, not appeals to character. Treat the gap between "I am open to feedback" and "I have integrated it" as a routine engineering problem — not a sign of bad faith.

The gap exists in everyone. Closing it is not a matter of being a better person — it is a matter of building structures that route information past the protective layer.

CHAPTER 5 OF 11

Communication

Intent that survives the cascade — and closes the loop.

Intent must survive five conditions: time compression, cognitive load, multi-level transmission, cross-cultural noise, and time-of-day degradation.

It rarely survives any of them by accident.

IN THIS CHAPTER

The Five Conditions Intent Must Survive
Why intent degrades — and what communication must withstand.

ITPE — Intent · Task · Purpose · End State
The structural communication of intent. Every assignment
carries the four elements field leaders need to act when the plan breaks.

Narrative — Making the Future Concrete
ITPE delivers structure. Narrative delivers texture. The two pair.

DTOF — The Delegation-to-Task Cascade
Six steps. Every line of effort traceable back through every step.

Walking the Line
Seven questions to a crew boss. Reveal whether intent landed —
or where in the cascade it broke.

Daily Rhythm — Pre-ops · Midday · Post-ops
Three meetings, three intents. Each is a tool, not a ritual.

Briefer's Checklist
Before · During · Close. The verification that ends the brief.

SAPPER
Successes · Adjustments · Problems · Plans · Equipment · Resources.

THE CHAPTER'S CLAIM

Intent does not survive a cascade unless the cascade was
designed to carry it — and the carrier was tested at each
handoff.

PARENT REFERENCE
OLFG Ch. 5, pages 225–262.

RELATED CHAPTERS
Ch. 1 (Mission Command) ·
Ch. 7 (Contingency & Adaptation)

WHY COMMUNICATION DESIGN MATTERS

The Five Conditions
Intent Must Survive

THE LESSON

Intent does not degrade randomly. It degrades under five
predictable conditions — each of which can be planned for.

1 · TIME COMPRESSION

What got said in a 20-minute brief degrades when the receiver has
30 seconds to act. The version that survives is the shortest one.

2 · COGNITIVE LOAD

Receivers under high load drop everything except the immediate task.
Intent is filtered out first. Anchor it to action, not to context.

3 · MULTI-LEVEL TRANSMISSION

Each handoff loses fidelity. Four levels of cascade and the original
intent is unrecognizable. Test at each level, not just the first.

4 · CROSS-CULTURAL NOISE

Different agencies, different jargon, different shorthand. The same
word means different things. The same silence means different things.

5 · TIME-OF-DAY DEGRADATION

Fatigue compresses cognitive bandwidth. Communication that worked
at 0700 will not work the same way at 1900. Plan for both.

*Design the brief, the cascade, and the rhythm to withstand all five.
Communication that ignores them is communication that will fail.*

TOOL · THE STRUCTURE OF INTENT

ITPE

Intent · Task · Purpose · End State.

THE LESSON

Communication structure for translating direction into field guidance. Every assignment carries the four elements field leaders need to act correctly when the plan breaks.

INTENT

Why this matters to the larger strategy.

The reason that survives when the plan does not. When conditions shift and the task is no longer feasible, the field leader uses intent to determine what to do instead.

TASK

What to accomplish.

Specific enough to act on, broad enough to permit adaptation in execution. Not a script — a destination with permitted improvisation about how to get there.

PURPOSE

How this task connects to the next echelon's mission.

The link that lets a subordinate make sound calls when conditions change. Without purpose, every shift in conditions becomes a request for guidance.

END STATE

What success looks like — observable, measurable.

The condition that tells the field leader the assignment is complete. "Contain the fire" is not an end state. "Defensible perimeter holds through the wind event" is.

VERIFY WITH A BACK-BRIEF

Have the receiver restate ITPE in their own words.
You are testing landing — not memory.

TOOL · THE TEXTURAL PAIR TO ITPE

Narrative

Making the future concrete.

THE LESSON

ITPE communicates the structure of intent. Narrative communicates its texture. A leader who pairs ITPE with a brief, concrete description of the future has communicated something the receiver will remember when the structure has faded.

FOUR FUNCTIONS

MAKE THE END STATE CONCRETE

"Containment by Friday" is a metric. "By Friday, defensible perimeter holds through the weekend wind event, residents are home, team transitions to a smaller organization" is a destination.

MAKE FAILURE CONSEQUENCES CONCRETE

In specific terms — what the public, cooperators, and community would experience if the plan fails. Sharpens every subsequent decision.

SURFACE UNSTATED ASSUMPTIONS

If you cannot narrate the future state concretely, the picture has not been formed. Diagnostic of your own thinking.

CONNECT WORK TO THE PEOPLE IT SERVES

Keeps the human consequences of success and failure visible.

THREE GUIDELINES — DISCIPLINE, NOT INDULGENCE

KEEP IT SHORT

Two or three sentences after ITPE. Long narratives become speeches.

KEEP IT CONCRETE

Specific places, specific people, specific consequences. Abstract narrative is indistinguishable from rhetoric.

KEEP IT HONEST

Routinely describing routine operations in catastrophic terms loses credibility for the moments that warrant catastrophic terms.

Structure may be filtered across the cascade. The picture is not.

TOOL · THE CASCADE

DTOF

Delegation-to-Task Framework.

THE LESSON
The sequence that connects strategic authority to daily tactical execution. Every step must be traceable both ways.

01 STEP

DELEGATION OF AUTHORITY

What the IMT is authorized to do — and what it is not.
Sets the boundary inside which everything else operates.

02 STEP

ISAP — STRATEGIC ALIGNMENT

Broad strategy generated through ideation with stakeholders.
Generates direction — not implementation. (See Ch. 2 p. 43.)

03 STEP

INCIDENT OBJECTIVES

Specific, measurable. Translate strategy into observable
conditions for this operational period.

04 STEP

LEADER'S INTENT (per division)

What effect to achieve, why, and within what constraints.
The reason that survives when the plan does not.

05 STEP

TASK · PURPOSE · END STATE

ITPE for each subordinate level. The structure of
communicated intent at every echelon.

06 STEP

LINES OF EFFORT

Daily accomplishments, resource needs, identified impacts.
Where strategic logic meets the operational period.

*If a division cannot trace daily work back through this cascade,
the chain is broken upstream. Symptoms appear at the bottom.
Cause sits higher.*

TOOL · VERIFYING INTENT LANDED

Walking the Line

THE LESSON

Back-briefs verify one handoff. Walking the line verifies
the result of the entire chain. Ask people on the line what
they understand — not what they were told.

SEVEN QUESTIONS · ASK A CREW BOSS, DIRECTLY

1 What is your task?
What you are doing right now.

2 What is the purpose of that task?
How it connects to the next echelon's mission.

3 What does success look like from where you are standing?
The end state, in observable terms.

4 What conditions would make the current plan invalid?
The triggers for escalation.

5 What are you expected to report immediately?
What rises without being asked.

6 What are you authorized to decide without asking?
The decision space.

7 What are you NOT authorized to commit without approval?
The half of the contract usually unstated.

READING THE ANSWERS

Coherent answers across all seven →
Intent has survived four or five handoffs. The cascade is working.

Confused answers →
Locate the level at which the cascade broke. The crew boss did not
fail. The handoff above them did.

DISCIPLINE · THREE MEETINGS, THREE INTENTS

Daily Rhythm

Pre-Ops · Midday · Post-Ops.

THE LESSON

Each meeting is a tool, not a ritual. If the meeting is not
producing what its intent demands, the meeting is failing.

PRE-OPS BRIEFING

DAY START

Confirm 204s are accurate. Synchronize on priorities.
Incorporate overnight intelligence. Time-compressed —
divisions brief in one to two minutes.

FAILURE MODE

What it must not become: a replay of the post-ops debrief.

MIDDAY UPDATE

OPERATIONAL PERIOD

Real-time progress against objectives. Resource needs
and 24-48-72 hour projections. Feeds the next IAP.
Without this, planning works from stale data.

FAILURE MODE

What it must not become: a status report with no decisions.

POST-OPS DEBRIEF

DAY END · SAPPER

Situation · Action · Purpose · Plan · Execution · Result.
Purpose is the element most often missing — without it, the
debrief becomes a timeline rather than a learning opportunity.

FAILURE MODE

What it must not become: a timeline recital without learning.

*A meeting that drifts from its intent does not just waste time.
It produces a synchronized misunderstanding.*

TOOL · THE OPERATIONAL BRIEFING

Briefer's Checklist

Before · During · Close.

THE LESSON

A brief is decisions, not deliveries. Time spent without naming the decisions is time the brief failed to do its work.

A · BEFORE THE BRIEF — PREPARATION

- ☐ I can name the type of brief — information, decision, synchronization, or mission preparation — and the receivers know which it is.
- ☐ Every slot in the brief earns its place by decision relevance.
- ☐ The decision (or set of decisions) the brief is supporting is named.
- ☐ Content already in the IAP has been cut unless it changes a decision today.
- ☐ The total brief fits the attention budget — target 10–15 minutes routine, never more than 20 without explicit justification.
- ☐ Triggers, thresholds, and decisions each forecast supports are named — not just the forecast itself.

B · DURING THE BRIEF — EXECUTION

- ☐ The type and purpose of the brief is named in the opening.
- ☐ Hierarchy is suppressed — contributors with decision-relevant information speak regardless of rank.
- ☐ Time is monitored against the attention budget. Long is not thorough.
- ☐ Questions are invited. Silence is not consent — it is data about landing.
- ☐ Unresolved issues are named in real time, not deferred indefinitely.

C · THE CLOSE — VERIFICATION

- ☐ The back-brief is performed — at scale, by cascade. Each echelon verifies.
- ☐ Every assignment has a named owner and a time.
- ☐ Re-brief triggers are identified — what changes would force us to re-convene?
- ☐ The brief ends with explicit decisions and actions — not handshakes and implicit understandings.

If every key participant can independently restate mission, intent, decision points, risks, and their own role — the brief succeeded.
If they cannot, it did not — regardless of how it appeared.

CHAPTER CLOSE · COMMUNICATION FAILURE PATTERNS

Watch For

When intent is degrading across your cascade.

Communication failures are rarely a single dropped message. They are patterns of degradation — predictable, recurring, and visible if you know where to look.

PATTERN · DIFFERENT PICTURES, SAME WORDS

Three division supervisors describe success differently.

- Each can articulate the task — but the end states they describe diverge.
- Resource priorities differ across divisions in ways the IAP does not explain.
- Each is sure they are doing what was asked. Each is doing something different.
- Back-briefs were performed. The divergence still happened.

Diagnosis: Structure was communicated; texture was not. ITPE without narrative.
Repair: Add narrative (p. 67). Walk the line (p. 69) to test where it landed.

PATTERN · INFORMATION DUMP IN PLACE OF BRIEF

The brief is long, comprehensive, and decision-free.

- Every section runs over time. Briefers compete for slots.
- Content already in the IAP is repeated verbally.
- Technical briefers drift into hyperbole or attention capture.
- No one can name what decisions the brief supported.

Diagnosis: Delivery without intent. Practice failure, not doctrine failure.
Repair: Apply the Briefer's Checklist (p. 71). Cut what does not change a decision.

PATTERN · CASCADE BREAKS QUIETLY

The crew boss cannot articulate what they are not authorized to commit.

- Questions 5–7 of Walking the Line produce silence or guesses.
- Reporting up is reactive — the leader hears about issues after they cascade.
- Field leaders ask for permission on routine calls. Or commit without asking.
- Decision space was implied, never named.

Diagnosis: Half a contract communicated. The right column is missing.
Repair: Re-issue ITPE with explicit decision-space boundaries (Ch. 1 p. 33).

SEE ALSO

Communication failures degrade everything downstream — execution, adaptation, learning. Most cascades into other chapters originate here. Section IV maps which patterns lead where.

TOOL · USEFUL UPWARD REPORTING HAS SIX ELEMENTS

What Field Leaders Owe Upward

A trainable discipline, not a personality trait. Each element compensates for a limitation an absent element would create.

THE LESSON

The senior leader's picture is only as good as what reaches it. A report that emphasizes what is going well, to stay safe, widens the gap between the picture and the ground until something forces a correction.

THE SIX ELEMENTS

01 OBSERVATION
What is actually happening, in concrete terms. "The south line is holding," not "we're in good shape."

02 INTERPRETATION
What the observation means, given conditions — the leader's judgment, which the next echelon evaluates.

03 RECOMMENDATION
What should happen next. Converts the field leader from a sensor into a decision contributor.

04 CHANGE FROM EXPECTED
What differs from what the plan assumed. Most often omitted, most consequential. Silence invalidates the strategy.

05 CALIBRATED UNCERTAINTY
What you know, suspect, and do not know. False certainty is a liability; honest uncertainty is a contribution.

06 WHAT IS NEEDED, BY WHEN
Specific and timestamped. Not "we may need water" but "we exceed capacity by 1400 unless tenders stage by 1300."

DISCIPLINE IN WHAT IS NOT REPORTED

Report what changes the picture, affects another element, crosses a threshold, or was requested. Routine confirmation needs no transmission. The absence of an exception is itself information.

Reports that include everything are equivalent to reports that include nothing — the senior leader cannot distinguish signal from noise.

CHAPTER 6 OF 11

Communication Discipline

Direct speech matched to operational consequence.

Communication failures in incident management are rarely failures of vocabulary. They are failures of discipline — the disciplined match of speech to operational requirement, of clarity to consequence, of register to risk.

Structural context determines speech register — not the other way around.

IN THIS CHAPTER

Requirements Not Possibilities
Operational language names what must be true, not what might happen. Vagueness shifts the cost of clarity from speaker to receiver.

Disambiguation
Before answering, surface the multiple meanings the question carries. The introducer owns the work of making a topic decidable.

Coordination Support
Coordination is an operational priority, not a courtesy. Treat its breakdowns as you would treat any other operational failure.

Mitigated Speech
Hedging language obscures urgency. Train the team to surface concerns at the strength of the actual risk — not the strength permitted by hierarchy.

THE CHAPTER'S CLAIM

Communication discipline is the daily practice that makes mission command operate.

The framework is built on speech; the speech is what fails first.

PARENT REFERENCE

OLFG Ch. 6, pages 263–292.

RELATED CHAPTERS

Ch. 5 (Communication) · Ch. 7 (Contingency)

DISCIPLINE · ASKING DECIDABLE QUESTIONS

Requirements, Not Possibilities

A topic raised as a possibility produces conversation. A topic raised as a requirement produces a decision.

THE LESSON

The introducer of the topic owns the work of making it decidable. Recognize when a topic needs a decision rather than a discussion, and introduce it in the form that produces the decision.

POSSIBILITY FRAMING	REQUIREMENT FRAMING
The topic enters as a possibility. Someone observes that a move might be useful.	**The introducer defines the requirement.** Stated as criteria the decision needs to meet.
The conversation is exploratory. It has no defined endpoint. It generates ideas and concerns.	**The decision authority is named.** Who owns the call is explicit before the conversation.
The room does the introducer's work. Participants without the expertise speculate on feasibility.	**The timeline is named.** By when the decision must be produced is explicit.
The cost accumulates. The topic returns each operational period, undecided.	**The conversation produces a decision.** The room evaluates the requirement against conditions.

THE SELF-AUDIT

Have I asked a question the receiver can act on — or one that requires them to figure out what I actually need before they can answer?

THREE ELEMENTS MAKE A TOPIC DECIDABLE

THE REQUIREMENT	DECISION AUTHORITY	THE TIMELINE
stated as criteria	*named explicitly*	*named explicitly*

The work is the same. The framing determines whether the conversation produces a decision or produces more conversation.

DISCIPLINE · NAME THE REFERENCE BEFORE YOU ANSWER

Disambiguation

When a phrase can resolve more than one way, name the specific reference before continuing the conversation.

THE LESSON

Two operators use the same phrase to mean different things. The conversation feels coherent. The cost surfaces hours or days later, when the gap between the two understandings becomes visible.

PHRASES THAT CARRY MORE THAN ONE REFERENCE

the grazing meeting   *the line*   *the crew*   *the plan*   *the intent*

THE CONSTRUCTION

which X — A or B?

THE DISCIPLINE WORKS IN BOTH DIRECTIONS

BEFORE YOU ANSWER	BEFORE YOU ASK
If a question contains a phrase with more than one reference, pause and name it before you answer. Confirm which one the asker means.	If you ask a question you recognize might be ambiguous, name the specific reference in the question itself — and save both of you the pause.

THE COST ASYMMETRY

The cost of asking: a two-to-five-second pause that names the reference. The cost of not asking: a missed meeting, a wrong plan executed, a coordination failure — a class of failures with no upper bound on cost.

The conversation where the ambiguity occurs is the cheapest place to fix it. Every conversation downstream of it is a place where the fix costs more.

DISCIPLINE · SEND THE EFFECT AND THE SUPPORT TOGETHER

Coordination Support

An operational decision rarely requires only the operational effect.
It also requires the support that makes the effect possible.

THE LESSON

Communicate the operational effect and the support requirement
together, in the same communication, in language that lets receivers
in different functions act on both.

TWO ELEMENTS, ONE COMMUNICATION

THE OPERATIONAL EFFECT		THE SUPPORT REQUIREMENT
What you need to accomplish.	**+**	What you need to accomplish it.

THE FAILURE MODE

The effect goes through one channel. The support goes through another —
different timing, different vocabulary, different scope. The mismatch
produces coordination failure at the moment of execution.

WHEN YOU DEVIATE, THE REQUIREMENT INCREASES

A deviation is a coordination event. Other functions are running
operations that assume the planned course. Communicate the deviation
immediately — same channel, same receivers, both elements named.

OWNERSHIP IS BIDIRECTIONAL

THE INTRODUCER	THE RECEIVER
Owns communicating both elements together — the effect and the support, in one communication.	Owns confirming both elements were received. Acknowledging only the effect leaves the support unowned.

A communication acknowledged only on the effect is partially complete —
and the receiver has accepted the part they did not address.

DISCIPLINE · SPEAK DIRECTLY WHEN THE SITUATION REQUIRES IT

Mitigated Speech

The corrective is not the absence of social skill. It is calibrated language — directness matched to operational consequence.

THE LESSON

Hedging, softening, and indirection added when the social context would make directness uncomfortable. The information is technically delivered — but under load, the receiver does not act on it.

CALIBRATE THE REGISTER TO THE CONSEQUENCE

TRIVIAL MATTERS	CONSEQUENTIAL MATTERS
Softened, conversational, socially attentive language is appropriate.	Directness proportional to the consequence is required.

The discipline is in the calibration — not in defaulting to one register.

THE SELF-AUDIT

Before hedging a message about an operational consequence, ask: would these hedges still be there if I were speaking to someone of lower standing? If they vanish downward, they are mitigated speech.

THE FAILURE MODE

The hazard is framed as a question, not a statement. The objection is framed as a consideration. The intelligence is hedged. The message arrives in a form that does not require action — so none is taken.

THE REFRAME

Mitigated speech is not a personal defect. It is the predictable result of cooperative socialization. Cooperation gets practiced; directness does not. It can be installed — but only deliberately and consistently.

The discipline of direct speech runs against the training. It can be installed, but the underlying defaults are pulling the opposite way every time.

CHAPTER 7 OF 11

Contingency

And the discipline to know when iteration is no longer enough.

Every plan will need to change. The question is whether you have built the capacity to change it — before the need becomes a crisis.

Leaders who do not build that capacity are not leading. They are betting.

IN THIS CHAPTER

Left of Bang — the Proactive Posture
Every hour spent before the event buys options after it.

Why Humans Are Bad at This
Six cognitive obstacles to contingency planning — and how to design around them rather than rely on willpower.

Contingency Framework
Six elements every contingency must have. Missing one and you have a hope, not a plan.

Planning Horizons
Plan to the level of detail conditions support — and no further.

Iteration vs. Adaptation
Iteration adjusts tactics within the strategy. Adaptation changes the strategy itself. The triggers are different.

Adaptation Triggers
The four conditions that warrant strategic reassessment — named in advance so you don't have to negotiate them mid-event.

THE CHAPTER'S CLAIM

Every hour spent left of bang buys options right of bang.
Every hour you do not invest narrows what's available later.

PARENT REFERENCE
OLFG Ch. 7, pages 293–322.

RELATED CHAPTERS
Ch. 2 (Strategic Thinking) ·
Ch. 3 (Red Teaming)

DISCIPLINE · THE PROACTIVE POSTURE

Left of Bang

THE LESSON

On a timeline where "bang" is the moment the adverse event occurs, everything to the left is proactive — preparing, positioning, identifying triggers before they fire.

TWO POSTURES

LEFT OF BANG	RIGHT OF BANG
Proactive — before the event.	*Reactive — after the event.*

LEFT OF BANG

WHAT IT LOOKS LIKE

Continuously scanning for changing conditions.

Identifying decision points before they arrive.

Pre-positioning resources and information.

Planning for events that may not happen — knowing the cost is trivial.

WHAT IT FEELS LIKE

Wasted effort — until the one time it is not.

PROTECTS
Options.

RIGHT OF BANG

WHAT IT LOOKS LIKE

Responding to events that have already occurred.

Whatever resources happen to be available are what you have.

Time pressure that did not exist when conditions were developing.

Fewer options, shorter time, more constrained decisions.

WHAT IT FEELS LIKE

Real work — and there is more of it than you can do.

PROTECTS
Nothing. You are inside the consequence.

THE EXCHANGE RATE

Every hour spent left of bang buys options right of bang. *Every hour you do not invest narrows the options when you need them most.*

COGNITIVE OBSTACLES

Why Humans Are Bad at Contingency Planning

THE LESSON

Contingency planning requires imagining futures that differ from the one you expect. Humans perform this task poorly.

CONFIRMATION BIAS

Search for, interpret, and remember information that confirms the current plan. Discount information that suggests it may fail.

ANCHORING

Initial assessment fixes attention. Difficult to adjust as conditions evolve — even when conditions clearly have.

OVERCONFIDENCE

Overestimate ability to predict what happens next. Reduces the perceived need for contingencies in the first place.

DESIRE FOR PREDICTABILITY

Uncertainty creates anxiety. Leaders treat the plan as more certain than it is — because certainty feels better than the alternative.

PATTERN MATCHING

Familiar pattern from past incident. Assume similar outcomes. But complex systems are path-dependent; the same inputs do not.

COGNITIVE LOAD

Holding multiple futures in mind requires effort. Under load, the team drops contingency work first — and the leader signals it's optional.

THE INTERVENTION THAT WORKS

Design around the obstacles — do not rely on willpower. *Deadlines. Named contingencies. Scheduled review. The discipline is structural — not personal.*

These are not character flaws. They are structural.

TOOL · SIX ELEMENTS, ALL REQUIRED

Contingency Framework

THE LESSON
Six elements every contingency must have. Missing one means
you have a hope — not a plan.

TRIGGER	The observable condition that activates the contingency. Specific enough that anyone watching can recognize it.
TIMELINE	How long from trigger to action — and whether resources can move in that window. The time test runs here.
RESOURCES	Identified, available, and committed. A contingency that depends on resources you do not control is a hope.
COORDINATION	Who is informed, by whom, in what sequence. Notification chain decided before the trigger fires, not improvised after.
AUTHORITY	Who decides to activate. Pre-authorized for routine contingencies; named decision-maker for consequential ones.
DOCUMENTATION	Where the plan lives so anyone activating it can find it. Briefed to executors before activation, not during it.

THE TIME TEST

1. What triggers this plan? Observable, measurable — not judgment.
2. How long does execution take from trigger? Include ordering, mobilization, travel, construction, rest.
3. How much time exists between trigger and need? If #2 > #3, the plan does not work. Move the trigger earlier, pre-position, or build a different plan.

DISCIPLINE · MATCH DETAIL TO CONDITIONS

Planning Horizons

THE LESSON

Plan to the level of detail conditions support — and no further. Anything beyond what you can foresee will be wrong. Time invested there is not invested in iteration.

0–24 HR *detailed tactical*	**DETAILED TACTICAL** Specific tasks, resources, assignments, and contingency triggers. Precision is possible — and required at this horizon.
24–48 HR *operational planning*	**OPERATIONAL PLANNING** Decision points identified, resource needs anticipated, alternative approaches outlined. Detailed enough to prepare; provisional enough to flex.
48 HR - 5 DAY *lines of effort*	**LINES OF EFFORT** Lines of effort with anticipated decision points. Broad resource projections. Key assumptions monitored. Contingency branches in concept.
BEYOND 5 DAY *strategic direction*	**STRATEGIC DIRECTION** Identified assumptions that must hold for strategy to remain viable. Conditions under which strategy would need to change. Nothing more detailed.

If your planning process produces the same level of detail for day seven that it produces for tomorrow, you are investing in fiction.

THE DISTINCTION THAT MATTERS

Iteration vs. Adaptation

THE LESSON

Iteration adjusts the tactics within the strategy. Adaptation changes the strategy itself. The triggers, the process, and the communication requirements are different.

TWO DIFFERENT KINDS OF CHANGE

ITERATION	ADAPTATION
Tactics change. Strategy holds.	*Strategy itself changes.*

ITERATION — Tactics change. Strategy holds.

TRIGGER

End of an operational period.
New information from execution.
Resource shifts within plan.

CADENCE

Daily — post-ops, planning,
pre-ops for the next day.

DECISION

Within the OSC's authority.
Inside the existing strategy.

COMMUNICATION

Normal channels. Standard rhythm.
No stakeholder briefing needed.

WHAT IT LOOKS LIKE

"We're shifting Div A resources to Div B for the wind event. Same plan, different distribution."

ADAPTATION — Strategy itself changes.

TRIGGER

Strategic assumption invalidated.
Resource picture fundamentally shifts.
Conditions outside what plan assumed.

CADENCE

When triggered — not on schedule.
Often forced by conditions, not chosen.

DECISION

Requires IC. May need agency
administrator concurrence.

COMMUNICATION

Re-brief at every echelon. Stakeholders.
Public communication may shift.

WHAT IT LOOKS LIKE

"Containment is no longer achievable. We're shifting to a defensive-perimeter strategy. New end state, new resources."

THE CONFUSION COSTS BOTH WAYS

Treating adaptation as iteration — strategy changes get under-communicated.
Treating iteration as adaptation — every small change becomes a crisis.
Name which one you are doing before you do it.

TOOL · WHEN THE STRATEGY MUST CHANGE

Adaptation Triggers

THE LESSON

Name the conditions that would warrant strategic change in advance — not in the middle of the event. Negotiating the trigger mid-event is how organizations fail to adapt at all.

RESOURCE COLLAPSE

The resource picture has shifted so dramatically that the current approach is no longer viable. Major demob, surge pulled, capability that anchored the plan is gone.
What the plan needed is no longer available.

CONDITION INVALIDATION

Fire behavior or weather has invalidated the operating concept. What the plan assumed about how the system would respond is not what is happening.
The model is wrong, not the execution.

STAKEHOLDER SHIFT

Agency administrator direction, political environment, or public priorities have changed in ways that alter what the operation is for.
The why has shifted, not just the how.

ASSUMPTION FAILURE

A load-bearing assumption — surfaced via KAC or premortem — has been proven wrong. The link between actions and end state no longer holds.
The chain breaks at the link, not the action.

WHEN ANY ONE FIRES — THE RESPONSE

Stop iterating. Re-issue ITPE at every echelon. Brief stakeholders.
Name the new strategy — and what about the old one no longer applies.

Watch For

When contingency and adaptation are failing.

Contingency failures are quiet. The team is busy. The plan is executing. The triggers no one set are not firing because no one is watching for them.

PATTERN · DETAILED PLANS FOR UNKNOWABLE FUTURES

Day seven gets the same detail as tomorrow.

- Specific tasks and resources assigned for periods conditions can't predict.
- Planning effort feels rigorous. The output ages out in 48 hours.
- The team feels prepared. They are prepared for the wrong scenarios.
- When conditions shift, the detailed plans are irrelevant.

Diagnosis: Detail beyond the horizon. Cognitive resources invested in fiction.
Repair: Apply Planning Horizons (p. 77). Redirect effort to iteration.

PATTERN · CONTINGENCIES WITHOUT TRIGGERS

The plan B exists on paper. No one knows when to activate it.

- Contingencies are documented but no triggers are specified.
- Triggers are subjective ("when conditions warrant") not observable.
- Time test was never run. Execution window may be shorter than build time.
- When the event occurs, the contingency is improvised, not activated.

Diagnosis: Plans without triggers are documentation, not preparation.
Repair: Six-element Contingency Framework (p. 76). Run the time test on each.

PATTERN · ITERATION WHEN ADAPTATION IS NEEDED

Daily tactical adjustments under a strategy that no longer fits.

- Every operational period brings new adjustments. None improve the picture.
- Load-bearing assumptions have failed. The plan continues anyway.
- Stakeholders sense the strategy is no longer working. The team has not said so.
- "Pregnant with the plan" — the strategy from Ch. 2 (p. 45).

Diagnosis: Iteration is being used to avoid the harder work of adaptation.
Repair: Apply Adaptation Triggers (p. 79). Name which one has fired.

SEE ALSO

Failures here cascade into Ch. 8 (AAR — where they should surface) and Ch. 2 (Strategy — where the original assumptions should have been more honestly tested).

CHAPTER 8 OF 11

AAR & Learning

The conditions, structure, and follow-through that turn lessons identified into lessons learned.

Most organizations identify lessons. Few learn them. The distance between identification and learning is where organizational behavior either changes or repeats.

The AAR is not a form, not a meeting type. It is a culture.

IN THIS CHAPTER

Psychological Safety
The non-negotiable precondition. Without it, every structure that follows produces sanitized output.

DEBrIEF Framework
Define · Engage · Background · review · Internal · External · Follow-up. The lowercase 'r' is intentional.

Public Learning vs. Private Correction
Match the venue to the function. Conflating them degrades all of them.

Work as Imagined / Done / Reported
Three layers. The gaps between them are where learning happens — and where it gets buried.

Just Culture
Honest error · negligence · recklessness. Without the distinction, every error is treated the same — and reporting stops.

From Lessons Identified to Lessons Learned
Eight inflection points. Stewardship is where the work most often fails — not in the analysis.

THE CHAPTER'S CLAIM

If the AAR feels safe to skip, the next failure is already paid for. The lesson was on the table — and no one carried it forward.

PARENT REFERENCE
OLFG Ch. 8, pages 323–356.

RELATED CHAPTERS
Ch. 4 (Decision Quality) ·
Ch. 9 (Team Cohesion)

THE NON-NEGOTIABLE PRECONDITION

Psychological Safety

THE LESSON

Without psychological safety, the AAR receives sanitized inputs and produces sanitized outputs. The organization learns from its preferred narrative, not its actual experience.

WHAT IT IS — AND IS NOT

WHAT IT IS	WHAT IT IS NOT
The shared belief that the team is safe for interpersonal risk-taking.	**Comfort. Niceness. The absence of accountability.**
• Honest reporting is welcomed, not penalized.	• Not freedom from critique — freedom from punishment for honesty.
• Mistakes are surfaced, examined, and used.	• Not lowered standards — higher standards, applied honestly.
• Dissent is heard before consensus is declared.	• Not a soft culture — a culture that holds harder things.
• Questions outnumber assertions.	• Not absence of consequence — proportional consequence (see p. 86).
Built daily. Lost in minutes.	*"Nice" cultures often produce nothing.*

HOW THE LEADER ESTABLISHES IT

GO FIRST

Open the AAR with a specific mistake you made. Not a rehearsed anecdote. A real error, described with enough detail that the team understands you are practicing honesty, not performing humility.

DEMAND SPECIFICS

"We communicated well" → "Give me the specific example." Generalities produce the feeling of reflection without the substance.

USE STRONG PERFORMERS AS SOURCE OF TEACHABLE MISTAKES

They have the standing to absorb public critique. The team learns that even the people they respect most make mistakes — normalizing the discussion of mistakes for everyone.

If the leader cannot share their own mistakes, the team will not share theirs.

TOOL · STRUCTURED REVIEW

DEBrIEF Framework

The lowercase "r" is intentional. The chronological timeline is the least valuable part. The learning lives in the other six steps.

D — **DEFINE**

Set duration. State the objectives of the response being reviewed. Anchor the discussion to what was supposed to happen.

E — **ENGAGE**

Create conditions for honest participation. Leader goes first, with a real mistake.

B — **BACKGROUND**

Pre-incident preparation. Plan clarity. Validated assumptions. Systemic problems live here — not in the timeline.

r — **review**

Chronological events. Brief. This is not where learning happens. Knowing what happened is not learning. Why it happened is.

I — **INTERNAL**

Team reflection — what we did, why it made sense at the time, what we would change. Specific, not general.

E — **EXTERNAL**

System factors — conditions, resources, organizational dynamics. Coordination and handoffs with external partners.

F — **FOLLOW-UP**

Assigned actions, owners, deadlines. Without this, the AAR was a conversation — not a working session.

Skipping a step degrades the process. Rushing the process tells the team that learning is a lower priority than moving on.

DISCIPLINE · MATCH VENUE TO FUNCTION

Public Learning ·
Private Correction

THE LESSON

AARs fail in two opposite ways. Public humiliation makes them dangerous; avoidance makes them performative. The standard is not "be nice." It is matching the venue to the function.

MATCH VENUE TO FUNCTION

PUBLIC LEARNING	Shared lessons. Use strong performers as the source where possible — they can absorb critique without losing standing, and the team learns that everyone makes mistakes.
PRIVATE CORRECTION	Difficult feedback for weaker performers. Specific. Developmental. With a path forward. Outside the AAR room.
PERFORMANCE COACHING	Sustained development conversation. Not an AAR. Different cadence, different rules.
FORMAL ACCOUNTABILITY	When evidence supports it. With process protection. Outside the learning environment.
MISCONDUCT REVIEW	Separate process. Different rules of evidence. Different people. Not in the AAR.

THE COMMON FAILURE

Conflating venues — using public learning to deliver private correction, or letting the AAR drift into accountability — *degrades all of them.*

THREE LAYERS · WHERE THE GAPS LIVE

Work as Imagined, Done, Reported

THE LESSON

Three layers describe the same operation. The gaps between them are the learning. The gaps are also the danger — when leaders mistake one layer for another.

01 IMAGINED
How the planner thought the work would be done.

What the plan says, what the briefing covered, what everyone assumed when they walked out the door.

Layer 1 of 3.

02 DONE
How the work actually happened.

What field leaders adapted in response to conditions, what the plan did not anticipate, what worked anyway.

Layer 2 of 3.

03 REPORTED
What gets written down — and what the organization later believes.

Not what happened. Not what got adapted. Not the gaps the field saw. Almost never the same as Done.

Layer 3 of 3.

WHERE LEARNING LIVES

Imagined-to-Done gap → the plan did not anticipate reality.
Done-to-Reported gap → honest reporting does not feel safe.
Both gaps are leverage points. Both are diagnostic.

PROPORTIONAL CONSEQUENCE

Just Culture

THE LESSON

Just culture distinguishes honest error from negligence from recklessness. Without the distinction, every error is treated the same way — and honest reporting stops.

HONEST ERROR

A reasonable person, with the same information and conditions, could have made the same call.
The locus of correction is the SYSTEM, not the individual.

RESPONSE

Coaching focuses on conditions that produced the error — workload, communication, information availability.

AT-RISK / NEGLIGENT

A reasonable person, with the same information and conditions, would not have made that call. Choices that increase risk, often normalized over time.

RESPONSE

Coaching and system redesign — not punishment alone. The behavior is the focus, not the outcome.

RECKLESSNESS

Knowing disregard for substantial and unjustifiable risk. The actor saw the risk, understood the consequence, chose to proceed.

RESPONSE

Discipline is appropriate. Process protections apply, but the consequence is proportional to the conscious choice, not the outcome.

A leader who made a sound decision that produced a bad outcome is not treated the same as one who ignored available information.

WHERE REVIEWS MOST OFTEN FAIL

From Lessons Identified
to Lessons Learned

THE LESSON

Most learning reviews fail not in the analysis but in the stewardship of what the analysis produced. A learning review passes through eight inflection points, in three groups.

THE EIGHT INFLECTION POINTS
GROUP 1 · ESTABLISHMENT — Set the conditions

1 CHARTER

Define scope, authority, and what the review is for.

2 METHOD

Choose analytical approach BEFORE evidence collection.

GROUP 2 · ANALYSIS — Do the work

3 RECONSTRUCTION

Rebuild the timeline from artifacts and traces.

4 DIAGNOSIS

Identify the conditions that produced the outcome.

5 DRAFTING

Translate findings into a coherent product.

GROUP 3 · STEWARDSHIP — Where reviews most often fail

6 TEAM SIGN-OFF

Authors confirm the draft reflects their analysis.

7 TRANSMITTAL

Draft moves to the convening authority for release.

8 PUBLICATION

Final product enters the institutional record.

REFRAME — THE ANALYTICAL DISCIPLINE INSIDE DEBrIEF

DEBrIEF is the structure. REFRAME is the analytical discipline applied within it.

PHASE 1 · RECONSTRUCT — Local rationality. What was knowable then.

PHASE 2 · DIAGNOSE — The conditions that produced the outcome.

PHASE 3 · TRANSLATE — Findings into change. The Stewardship phase.

Tier 1 reviews use Phase 1. Tier 2 (formal Learning Reviews) use all three.

WHERE WELL-CONDUCTED REVIEWS DIE

The team that did the analysis is not the team that controls the final document. Stewardship is where lessons identified become lessons learned — or do not.

CHAPTER CLOSE · WHEN AARs FAIL

Watch For

When learning is being staged, not produced.

An AAR that fails rarely announces it. The team holds the meeting, signs the report, and walks out unchanged. These are the patterns to watch — and the repair for each.

PATTERN · NO ONE GOES FIRST

The leader skips their own mistake. The team takes the signal.

- The Engage step is a quick acknowledgment, not a real disclosure.
- Discussion stays at the level of "what the team did well."
- No one names a specific decision they would do differently.

Repair: Leader names their own error first, specifically. Reset the floor.

PATTERN · TIMELINE SUBSTITUTES FOR LEARNING

The chronological "review" consumes the meeting.

- Most of the AAR is spent reconstructing what happened.
- Internal/External steps get five minutes each at the end.
- Follow-Up is "we'll send the notes out."

Repair: Cap the review step. Most learning lives in Internal, External, Follow-up.

PATTERN · INSIGHTS WITHOUT OWNERS

Lessons identified. Nothing assigned. AAR becomes a conversation.

- Recommendations are listed without a name attached.
- Deadlines are "soon" or "next season."
- No mechanism for verifying the change was made.

Repair: Every change → owner, deadline, verification. By name. Before the AAR ends.

PATTERN · DOCUMENT SOFTER THAN ANALYSIS

The published report is softer than the team's actual analysis.

- Findings narrowed between draft and publication.
- Hedges removed; uncertainty becomes assertion.
- Scope substituted. Defensive insertions appear in high-salience locations.

Repair: Stewardship phase (p. 87). Compare team draft to final. Document the changes.

SEE ALSO

Learning failures cascade into Ch. 9 (Team Cohesion — where the team stops believing reports matter) and Ch. 10 Evaluation — where the same behaviors get scored as "lessons learned" without behavior change).

CHAPTER 9 OF 11

Team Cohesion

Trust as operational enabler — not value statement.
The deliberate work that produces cohesion under stress.

Trust is what permits decentralized execution under stress. Without it, mission command degrades into freelancing or decision inertia.

The team sees what is tolerated — and adjusts.

IN THIS CHAPTER

Trust as Enabler — Three Dimensions
Interpersonal, cognitive, group-based. Each is built differently — and fails differently when absent.

Standing vs. Ad Hoc Teams
Standing teams accumulate trust over time. Ad hoc teams must build it under load. The difference is operational.

Counterproductive Leadership — Four Categories
Abusive · Self-Serving · Erratic · Incompetent. Each has observable indicators. The team sees what is tolerated.

Fairness Over Niceness
Cohesive teams require fairness, not niceness. Honest feedback, consistent standards, accountability without favorites.

The "We All Decided" Problem
When no individual owns the decision, the team learns nothing from the outcome — good or bad.

THE CHAPTER'S CLAIM

Cohesion takes years to build. It takes one leader behaving badly, tolerated, to destroy it. The *destruction is faster than the investment.*

PARENT REFERENCE
OLFG Ch. 9, pages 357–374.

RELATED CHAPTERS
Ch. 1 (Mission Command) ·
Ch. 8 (AAR & Learning)

TOOL · THREE DIMENSIONS

Trust as Enabler

THE LESSON

Effective teams require all three dimensions of trust.
Each is built through different mechanisms, and each fails
in a different way when absent. They compound — but do not substitute.

01 INTERPERSONAL	02 COGNITIVE	03 GROUP-BASED
Knowing the person	*Knowing the work*	*Sharing the patch*
BUILT THROUGH	**BUILT THROUGH**	**BUILT THROUGH**
Direct personal interaction over time. Shared experience, common humor, the small reps that make someone known as a person — not just as a role.	Demonstrated reliability and competence under load. Confidence that the person in the next position will do their job — and do it well.	Membership in a recognized in-group — your team, your agency, your profession. Implicit, default trust that comes with the patch.
WITHOUT IT	**WITHOUT IT**	**WITHOUT IT**
Teams respect each other's competence but cannot communicate openly. Disagreements stay buried.	Teams that like each other but cannot rely on each other. Coordination falters at the first hard problem.	Nothing. This is the weakest form — what assembled strangers start with. Enough to begin work; not enough to sustain it.

*Trust is not a value statement. It is what permits
decentralized execution under stress.*

THE OPERATIONAL CONSEQUENCE

Standing teams have all three. Ad hoc teams arrive with
group-based trust only — and must build the other two under load.

TRUST ACCUMULATION DIFFERENCE

Standing vs. Ad Hoc

THE LESSON

Standing teams accumulate trust over time. Ad hoc teams must build it under load — when energy is needed for the mission, not for team formation. The difference is operationally significant.

THE DIFFERENCE — STARTING CONDITIONS

STANDING TEAMS — Trust already accumulated	AD HOC TEAMS — Trust must be built under load
WHAT THEY START WITH	**WHAT THEY START WITH**
Interpersonal trust from prior reps.	Group-based trust — the patch.
Cognitive trust calibrated through multiple incidents.	Procedural alignment — ICS, the shared doctrine.
Shared mental models — vocabulary, cadences, expectations.	No interpersonal or cognitive trust. Those are built — or they are not.
OPERATIONAL ADVANTAGE	**OPERATIONAL DEMAND**
Decentralized execution faster. Initiative recognized as initiative, not as freelancing.	Deliberate onboarding. Naming the work-style differences. Building shared mental models early.
The team that has worked together before does not need to learn each other under load.	*Treating an ad hoc team as if it were standing produces brittleness that only shows up under stress.*

THE OPERATIONAL MOVE

Onboard ad hoc members deliberately. Not "welcome aboard" — but a structured 30-minute conversation about how this *team works, what is expected, what to push back on.*

FOUR CATEGORIES · OBSERVABLE INDICATORS

Counterproductive Leadership

Each category is diagnosable through observable indicators. The team sees what is tolerated. Naming the pattern is the first move toward addressing it.

ABUSIVE

Belittling, public humiliation, threats, retaliation. Most visible category — and often the easiest to identify.

OBSERVABLE INDICATORS

- Berating others for mistakes
- Creating unnecessary conflict
- Ridiculing subordinates
- Retaliating against pushback

TEAM EFFECT

Trust destroyed immediately. A single instance reshapes every subsequent interaction.

SELF-SERVING

Personal advancement prioritized over mission or team. Credit for successes, blame deflected for failures.

OBSERVABLE INDICATORS

- Taking credit for others' work
- Distorting information to favor own ideas
- Personal accomplishment over team
- Narcissistic patterns

TEAM EFFECT

Members learn the leader's interests take precedence. They adjust — sycophantic or disengaged.

ERRATIC

Inconsistent standards, unpredictable reactions, decisions reversed without explanation. The team cannot calibrate.

OBSERVABLE INDICATORS

- Blaming others for own failures
- Volatile composure
- Inconsistent words and actions
- Paranoia or defensiveness

TEAM EFFECT

Cannot develop shared mental models. Cognitive resources go to managing the leader, not the incident.

INCOMPETENT

Lack of experience, willful neglect, or refusal to develop. Hard to address — requires acknowledging a placement error.

OBSERVABLE INDICATORS

- Unengaged, passive leadership
- Poor judgment under pressure
- Failure to communicate expectations
- Refusal to listen to subordinates

TEAM EFFECT

Often masked by abusive or self-serving behavior. Compounds the other categories.

Building cohesion takes years. Destroying it requires one leader behaving badly — tolerated.

TWO PAIRED DISCIPLINES

Fairness Over Niceness
& the "We All Decided" Problem

FAIRNESS OVER NICENESS — THE STANDARD THAT BUILDS TEAMS

Cohesive teams require fairness, not niceness. Niceness avoids hard conversations. Fairness has them — directly, specifically, with respect.

WHAT FAIRNESS LOOKS LIKE

- Consistent standards applied equally — regardless of relationship.
- Honest feedback delivered with respect — not weakened to preserve comfort.
- Accountability that does not depend on personal relationships.
- Disagreement and respect held simultaneously — not seen as a contradiction.

WHAT NICENESS LOOKS LIKE

- Hard conversations avoided. Feedback softened until the message is lost.
- Standards bent to preserve relationships. Inconsistency over time.

THE "WE ALL DECIDED" PROBLEM — ACCOUNTABILITY DIFFUSION

When a decision produces a bad outcome, "we all decided" is the response that no individual owns. Decisions without an owner produce no learning.

HOW IT APPEARS

- Group consensus replaces named decision authority.
- Dissent in the room dissolves once the meeting ends.
- After-action discussion uses "we" for failures, individual names for successes.
- No record of who made the call, on what reasoning, with what dissent.

THE REPAIR

- Name the decision-maker BEFORE the decision. Not after.
- Capture dissenting views in the record. Future learning depends on it.
- Document reasoning, not just the choice. Process, not outcome.
- In evaluation: "Who decided, on what basis, with what dissent?" — not "What happened?"

"We all decided" is how decisions become orphans. Orphan decisions cannot teach.

CHAPTER CLOSE · WHEN COHESION IS DEGRADING

Watch For

When trust is eroding and no one has named it.

Team failures rarely show up as a single event. They accumulate through small signals. These are the patterns to watch — and the immediate repair for each.

PATTERN · COORDINATED INDIVIDUALLY, NOT COLLECTIVELY

The team is competent person-by-person but does not act as a team.

- Communication is formal and guarded.
- Members do their part without coordinating across parts.
- The plan covers individual roles but no one tracks the seams.

Repair: Build shared mental models early. Ad hoc onboarding (p. 91).

PATTERN · COUNTERPRODUCTIVE LEADERSHIP TOLERATED

A leader behaves badly. The system does not act.

- Team members report the behavior privately, never publicly.
- The leader is shielded because of operational tempo or seniority.
- The pattern is named in private and excused in public.

Repair: Name the category (p. 92). Act on it. The team sees what is tolerated.

PATTERN · FEEDBACK ABSENT OR PRAISE-ONLY

Hard conversations are not happening. Niceness is being prioritized.

- Feedback is delivered only as praise — generic or specific.
- Standards bent to preserve relationships. Consistency erodes.
- The strong performer is held to a different standard than the weak.

Repair: Fairness over niceness (p. 93). Apply standards consistently.

PATTERN · NO ONE OWNS THE DECISION

"We all decided" emerges when something goes wrong.

- No name attached to the decision in the record.
- Dissent in the meeting did not survive into the documentation.
- "We" used for the failure; specific names appear only for credit.

Repair: Name the decision-maker before the call. Capture dissent.

SEE ALSO

Cohesion failures cascade into Ch. 1 (Mission Command — without trust, decentralization breaks) and Ch. 8 (AAR — reports go through the team's filter, and the filter shapes what is learnable).

CHAPTER 10 OF 11

Evaluating Performance

Measure capability rather than compliance.

Evaluation systems drift toward what is easy to measure. Compliance is easy. Capability is harder — and is what the operating environment actually demands.

What gets measured shapes what gets developed.

IN THIS CHAPTER

Two Opposing Evaluation Failures
Generous evaluation produces nothing actionable.
Punitive evaluation drives people away from hard assignments.

Dreyfus Progression — Novice to Expert
Five stages with different developmental needs. Treating an advanced beginner like an expert produces brittleness.

Behaviorally Anchored Scales
Specific observable behaviors at each performance level.
Replaces "meets expectations" with defensible feedback.

Capability vs. Compliance
Did they follow the process? — vs. — Did they exercise the judgment the situation required?

The Uniformity Trap
Standardized configurations measured instead of capability.

THE CHAPTER'S CLAIM

Self-evaluation is unreliable. Especially at advanced beginner — where confidence outpaces capability. The *system has to do the calibration work, not the leader.*

PARENT REFERENCE
OLFG Ch. 10, pages 375–396.

RELATED CHAPTERS
Ch. 4 (Decision Quality) ·
Ch. 8 (AAR & Learning)

FRAMING · OPPOSING FAILURES

Two Opposing Evaluation Failures

THE LESSON

Evaluation systems can fail in two opposite directions. Both produce the same downstream consequence: the system cannot tell who is ready for the next-harder assignment.

GENEROUS
Everyone meets expectations

WHAT IT LOOKS LIKE

"Meets expectations" is the default.

No specifics about what was done well or poorly.

Distinctions disappear. Strong and weak performers receive the same rating.

DOWNSTREAM COST

Developmental feedback absent. People cannot calibrate to the actual standard.

The system promotes people based on tenure and sign-offs, not capability.

The next high-complexity incident reveals what the evaluation hid.

PUNITIVE
Evaluation becomes career risk

WHAT IT LOOKS LIKE

A negative evaluation ends a career.

No recognized space between "ready" and "out of the pipeline."

Honest feedback is gateway to consequence, not to development.

DOWNSTREAM COST

People avoid difficult assignments where an honest evaluation might surface gaps.

The system measures who took the safer path, not who built the harder capability.

Risk-averse selection produces a thinner bench of high-complexity leaders.

THE STANDARD

An evaluation owes the person evaluated: specifics about what was done well, specifics about what was not, and a developmental *path from current to next level.*

MODEL · DEVELOPMENTAL STAGES

Dreyfus Progression

THE LESSON

Five stages of skill acquisition. Each has different developmental needs. Treating an advanced beginner like an expert produces brittleness. Treating an expert like a novice produces stagnation.

01 NOVICE

Rule-following. Cannot adapt to context.

WHAT THIS STAGE NEEDS

Needs structure and direct instruction. Apply the procedure as written.

02 ADVANCED BEGINNER

Recognizes situational features but still applies rules.

WHAT THIS STAGE NEEDS

Needs exposure to varied conditions. ⚠ Most miscalibrated stage — confidence outpaces capability.

03 COMPETENT

Plans deliberately. Sees relevance of features but still effortful.

WHAT THIS STAGE NEEDS

Needs feedback on judgment, not just task completion.

04 PROFICIENT

Pattern recognition operates intuitively. Sees situations as wholes.

WHAT THIS STAGE NEEDS

Needs reflective practice and red teaming.

05 EXPERT

Intuitive grasp. Acts without explicit deliberation in familiar conditions.

WHAT THIS STAGE NEEDS

Needs novel exposure and structured challenge to avoid drift.

*Self-evaluation is unreliable. Most unreliable at Advanced Beginner —
where the leader has just enough to see patterns, and not enough to see what they miss.*

TOOL · DEFENSIBLE FEEDBACK

Behaviorally Anchored Scales

THE LESSON

Three-point evaluation using specific observable behaviors at each performance level. Replaces "meets expectations" generality with specific, defensible, useful feedback.

HOW TO BUILD THEM

1. Identify the capability being evaluated.
e.g., "communicating intent" — not "communication skills."

2. Define what poor performance looks like — specific behaviors observed.
"Briefs task without purpose; receiver cannot adapt when conditions change."

3. Define acceptable performance — specific behaviors observed.
"Delivers ITPE; verifies through back-brief; receiver can restate purpose."

4. Define excellent performance — specific behaviors observed.
"Receiver articulates how they would adapt under three different conditions."

5. Evaluate against the anchors, not against an idealized standard.
If the anchor is the standard, the evaluation is defensible to the person evaluated.

WHAT AN EVALUATION OWES THE PERSON EVALUATED

SPECIFICS ABOUT WHAT WAS DONE WELL

Named behaviors, observed in named situations. Not "good communication."

SPECIFICS ABOUT WHAT WAS NOT

Named behaviors observed below the anchor. Without specificity, no calibration.

A DEVELOPMENTAL PATH

From current performance to next level. What to practice, where, with whom.

"Meets expectations" tells the person evaluated nothing they can use. Specifics make the next level visible.

TWO PAIRED DISCIPLINES

Capability vs. Compliance
& the Uniformity Trap

CAPABILITY vs. COMPLIANCE — WHAT ACTUALLY GETS MEASURED

COMPLIANCE

Did they follow the process? Yes / no.
Easy to measure. Easy to defend. Easy to document.
A leader who follows the process perfectly in a situation the process did not anticipate is compliant — and may still produce a bad outcome.

CAPABILITY

Did they exercise the judgment the situation required?
Hard to measure. Requires evaluator judgment.
The right thing to measure — and what the operating environment demands.

THE UNIFORMITY TRAP — MEASURING THE EASY THING

Evaluation systems drift toward standardized configurations because they can be checked against a checklist. Capability cannot. Over time, the system starts to mistake "follows the standard configuration" for "is capable."

HOW IT APPEARS

• Teams configured to look identical to other rostered teams — same titles, same structure — without checking that the people in the roles can do them.

• Evaluation focuses on whether the configuration meets the standard, not on whether the people in it perform under the actual conditions.

• Performance across operational tempos goes unmeasured. A leader competent at low tempo may not be ready for high.

Evaluate against assignment demands, not team self-image.

THE OPERATIONAL CONSEQUENCE

When the system measures the easy thing, it produces leaders who excel at the easy thing — and the system finds out what was missing when the conditions stop being easy.

Watch For

When the system measures the wrong thing.

Evaluation failures rarely produce visible symptoms — until the next high-complexity incident reveals the gap. These are the patterns to watch — and what to do about each.

PATTERN · EVALUATOR-CAPABILITY GAP

The evaluator has not credibly operated at the level being assessed.

- The evaluator has not been tested by the conditions that distinguish the role.
- Sees what compliance looks like; cannot see what capability looks like.
- Evaluations confirm the team's self-assessment.

Repair: Match evaluator experience to level. Mark the evaluation when match is absent.

PATTERN · GENERIC FEEDBACK

"Meets expectations" with no specifics about what was done well or poorly.

- The evaluation reads the same for everyone who completed the assignment.
- No developmental path identified. No next steps named.
- The strong performer and the marginal performer receive identical write-ups.

Repair: Behaviorally anchored scales (p. 98). Named behaviors in named situations.

PATTERN · DUNNING-KRUGER AT ADVANCED BEGINNER

A leader expresses confidence calibrated to a simpler environment.

- Confidence in readiness for high complexity, based on low-complexity exposure.
- Self-assessment treats success in simple incidents as proof of capability.
- The conditions that would reveal the gap have not been encountered.

Repair: Structured exposure to higher complexity (p. 97). Mentorship from above level.

PATTERN · UNIFORMITY OVER CAPABILITY

The system measures standardized configurations, not demonstrated capability.

- Teams scored on whether the roster matches the standard configuration.
- Successes celebrated without examining whether the process was sound.
- Failures investigated; successes not. Asymmetric rigor.

Repair: Capability over compliance (p. 99). Scrutinize successes with same rigor.

SEE ALSO

Evaluation failures cascade into Ch. 1 (Mission Command — leader-task fit depends on accurate capability assessment) and Ch. 8 (AAR — process evaluation requires the same discipline as performance evaluation).

CHAPTER 11 OF 11

Cognitive Readiness

Bias, stress, fatigue, and overload as predictable constraints on judgment — not personal failures.

Human cognition has limits. They are knowable, measurable, and predictable. Leaders who treat them as discipline problems will keep being surprised. Leaders who plan for them protect the instrument that everything else depends on.

The leader's cognition is the instrument. Manage it like one.

IN THIS CHAPTER

Acute vs. Chronic Stress
Acute stress is short-term and mobilizing. Chronic stress is sustained and depleting. Day one ≠ day ten.

Fatigue
The performance impairment you cannot see — because it degrades the capacity to recognize impairment.

Cognitive Load — Three Types
Intrinsic · Extraneous · Germane. Extraneous is the only one that is system-imposed waste. Attack it.

Endsley's Three Levels of SA
Perception · Comprehension · Projection. Each builds on the prior. Most failures are at Level 3 — not Level 1.

Bias Under Operational Conditions
Authority, confirmation, sunk-cost, and others amplified by stress.

THE CHAPTER'S CLAIM

You cannot will your way through cognitive overload any more than you can will your way through a broken leg. *It is a capacity problem, not a motivational one.*

PARENT REFERENCE
OLFG Ch. 11, pages 397–412.

RELATED CHAPTERS
Ch. 3 (Red Teaming) ·
Ch. 9 (Team Cohesion)

PHYSIOLOGY · TWO REGIMES

Acute vs. Chronic Stress

THE LESSON

Stress is designed to move you. Acute stress mobilizes; chronic stress depletes. The day-one leader is not the day-ten leader — not from lack of discipline, but from physiology.

ACUTE STRESS
Adrenaline · Mobilizing · Short-term

THE BIOLOGY

Adrenaline-based mobilization.

Enhances immune surveillance.
Sharpens attention.
Accelerates reaction time.

WHEN IT WORKS

In time-limited crises. The first hours of an incident. Acute structure fires, structure protection actions, rapid evacuations.

Acute stress is an asset when the demand is intense and brief.

The body is built for this — for minutes and hours, not weeks.

CHRONIC STRESS
Cortisol · Depleting · Sustained

THE BIOLOGY

Cortisol-based endurance response.

Suppresses immune function.
Degrades memory consolidation.
Impairs cognitive flexibility.

WHAT IT DEGRADES

Nuanced, context-dependent thinking — exactly what complex environments demand.

By day ten, the leader who arrived sharp and energized may be cognitively impaired — and not know it.

The body is not built for this. The leader has to build the discipline.

THE OPERATIONAL CONSEQUENCE

The wildfire assignment is not an acute stress event. It is a chronic one. Recovery is not weakness — it is the discipline *that protects the instrument the team depends on.*

THE IMPAIRMENT YOU CANNOT SEE

Fatigue

THE LESSON

Fatigue impairs the cognitive functions needed to recognize impairment. Fatigued leaders feel like they are performing adequately — because the same fatigue that is degrading their performance is degrading their self-assessment.

WHAT FATIGUE DEGRADES — OFTEN INVISIBLY

- **Narrowed attention.** The leader fixates on one problem while others go unaddressed.

- **Slowed processing.** Decisions take longer, with less of the consideration they used to receive.

- **Fixation on irrelevant detail.** Disproportionate energy on minor issues while major ones drift.

- **Reduced creative problem-solving.** The novel solution that was obvious on day three is invisible on day ten.

- **Eroded self-assessment.** The leader feels like they are performing — and is wrong.

WHAT TO DO — IT IS NOT MOTIVATIONAL

PLAN FOR SLEEP, DO NOT HOPE FOR IT

Sleep is the only intervention that meaningfully reverses fatigue. Schedule it. Protect it. A single night of restorative sleep does not repair multi-day deficit.

USE THE TEAM AS THE INSTRUMENT

When your self-assessment is degraded, the team's assessment of you is more reliable than your own. Ask. Listen. Trust their reading.

DELEGATE BEFORE YOU BREAK

A rested deputy outperforms a depleted commander. The discipline is recognizing this BEFORE the day where the depletion produces a bad call.

Fatigue is not a discipline problem. It is degraded equipment —
and the equipment is your cognition.

MODEL · THREE TYPES OF LOAD

Cognitive Load

THE LESSON

Mental capacity is finite. Three types of load consume it.
Two are unavoidable. One is system-imposed waste — and
that is the leverage point.

01 INTRINSIC
Inherent to the task

The complexity that lives in the work itself — a multi-division incident,
changing weather, competing stakeholder demands, time pressure. Cannot be reduced.

MANAGE

Match the task to a leader whose capability fits the intrinsic load.
Train. Build exposure. Develop the schema in advance.

02 EXTRANEOUS
Imposed by the system

Load imposed by how information is presented or how the system operates.
Poor briefings. Micromanagement. Low-quality documentation. Conflicting direction.

ATTACK

This is the load that adds no value. Eliminate it.
Clear briefings. Tight documentation. Delegation. Single sources of authority.

03 GERMANE
Builds capability

Load that builds pattern recognition, mental models, and schema.
Productive processing. The cognitive work of becoming a better leader.

PROTECT

Reserve time and attention for this. It is the only load that compounds.
Reflective practice. Red teaming. Mentorship. After-action review.

*Every unnecessary meeting, every unclear communication, every poorly
designed process adds extraneous load to leaders who can least afford it.*

MODEL · ENDSLEY · THREE LEVELS

Situational Awareness

THE LESSON

Three levels of situational awareness. Each level depends on
the one below. Most SA failures are not perception failures —
they are projection failures built on weak comprehension.

01 PERCEPTION
What is happening?

Reading the data — fire behavior, weather, resources,
positions. The intake of relevant information.

FAILURE MODE

Missing data, not misreading it. Critical information was
not perceived — either unavailable, or filtered out by
attentional narrowing under stress.

02 COMPREHENSION
What does it mean?

Integrating perceived elements into a coherent picture.
The leap from 'I see this' to 'this means that.'

FAILURE MODE

Information perceived but not understood. The leader sees
the data but does not recognize the pattern, the implication,
or the interaction between factors.

03 PROJECTION
What happens next?

Anticipating future state from current trajectory.
Where most operational decisions live.

FAILURE MODE

Leader understands the present but cannot project forward.
Managing the current situation while losing the future. Where
biases bite hardest.

Self-check: which level am I operating at right now?
If you cannot answer Level 3, you are reacting — not deciding.

WHEN BIASES BITE HARDEST

Bias Under Operational Conditions

THE LESSON

Cognitive biases that produce small errors in everyday conditions produce consequential ones under stress, fatigue, and time pressure. The biases that need watching change as conditions degrade.

AUTHORITY BIAS

Deference to the most senior person in the room.
Amplified by fatigue — cognitive depletion defaults to hierarchy.

When you hear it: "Whatever the chief decides."

CONFIRMATION BIAS

Searching for evidence that supports the forming conclusion.
Amplified when conclusions feel urgent. The first hypothesis becomes the only one.

When you hear it: "That confirms what we thought."

SUNK-COST

Persisting with a plan because of what has already been invested.
Amplified by ego and visibility — adapting feels like admitting waste.

When you hear it: "We've come this far."

ANCHORING

Over-weighting the first piece of information received.
Amplified by time compression — the early frame becomes the only frame.

When you hear it: "At first they said..." — and the team is still acting on that.

AVAILABILITY

Judging the likelihood of a scenario by how easily examples come to mind.
Amplified by recent vivid experience — last fire becomes this fire.

When you hear it: "This is just like [the recent event]."

The biases are not the problem. The conditions that amplify them are.
Knowing this lets you build the offsets in advance — see Ch. 3.

THE SLOW DRIFT

Normalization of Deviance

THE LESSON

Practices that would have been unacceptable on day one become routine by day ten. Standards erode incrementally — without a deliberate decision and without anyone noticing.

HOW IT HAPPENS

DAY 1

A small deviation occurs. It works out. No consequence.
The team's calibration shifts. The previous standard is now the conservative one.

DAY 3

A slightly larger deviation. Still works out. Still no consequence.
The new behavior is anchored as the new norm. The original standard is "old school."

DAY 7

A new team member arrives and is briefed on the current practice.
They never learn what the original standard was. The deviation is institutionalized.

There was no day on which someone decided to lower the standard.

THE COUNTER — PERIODIC RECALIBRATION

ASK THE DAY-ONE QUESTION

"Would I accept this practice if it appeared in front of me on day one?"
If the answer is no, the standard has drifted — even if today's team accepts it.

USE NEW ARRIVALS AS CALIBRATION INSTRUMENTS

Their reaction to current practice — before they adapt — surfaces drift that established members no longer see.

SCHEDULE EXPLICIT STANDARD REVIEWS

Mid-assignment, compare current practice to the briefed standard. The gap tells you where deviance has normalized.

The organization believes what leaders tolerate.
The standard is what gets enforced — not what gets briefed.

CHAPTER CLOSE · INSTRUMENT FAILURE

Watch For

When the leader's cognition is degrading and no one is naming it.

Cognitive readiness failures rarely show up as performance declarations. They show up in patterns of behavior that the degraded leader cannot reliably perceive in themselves.

PATTERN · FATIGUE WORN AS A BADGE

The leader is degrading their own instrument.

- Working 16–18 hour days and dismissing concerns about rest.
- Quality of briefings and decisions is visibly declining.
- Sleep and recovery framed as weakness rather than discipline.

Repair: Schedule recovery (p. 103). Delegate before the breaking point.

PATTERN · TUNNEL VISION

Attention narrows. The leader fixates on one problem while others go unaddressed.

- Disproportionate energy on a single problem or data point.
- Relevant information from other quarters going unprocessed.
- SA Level 3 is lost. The leader is reacting, not deciding.

Repair: Reduce load — delegate, simplify, prioritize (p. 104). Restore Level 3.

PATTERN · DEFAULTING TO HIERARCHY

Decisions made by the most senior person without input.

- Subordinates have stopped offering alternatives.
- Authority bias amplified by fatigue and time pressure.
- Cognitive depletion produces deference, not dialogue.

Repair: Designated challenger (Ch. 3 p. 53). Counter the bias structurally.

PATTERN · DRIFT BY DAY TEN

Practices unacceptable on day one are routine. No one noticed when it shifted.

- Standards eroded incrementally without deliberate decision.
- New arrivals are briefed on current practice, not original standard.
- "We've always done it this way" — even when "always" means day three.

Repair: Day-one question (p. 107). Use new arrivals as calibration instruments.

SEE ALSO · END OF SECTION III

Cognitive readiness underwrites every other capability. When this degrades, the others degrade with it. Section IV maps how the patterns across all ten chapters cascade — and where to look first when they do.

SECTION IV

Diagnostic Index

Symptom-to-cause translation. Start with what you observe. Find where to look next.

HOW TO USE THIS SECTION

Leaders rarely experience dysfunction as a chapter topic. They experience it as a symptom — the team is not performing, the plan keeps failing, communication is breaking down, decisions are being delayed.

This section translates observable symptoms into probable causes — and points to the chapters that address them.

THE METHOD — TREAT THE FIRST MATCH AS A HYPOTHESIS

1 · IDENTIFY THE SYMPTOM

Find the entry in WHAT YOU OBSERVE that best matches what you see.

2 · READ THE PROBABLE CAUSE AS A HYPOTHESIS

Not certainty. The diagnosis you are testing against further observation.

3 · GO TO THE REFERENCED CHAPTER

Apply the framework. Test whether the hypothesis explains what you see.

4 · IF THE DIAGNOSIS DOES NOT PRODUCE IMPROVEMENT, LOOK UPSTREAM

The cause is rarely where the symptom appears.

THE SEVEN DOMAINS

Symptoms rarely respect domain boundaries. Cross-references appear at each spread.

Strategy & Direction

DOMINANT DEMAND
Strategic clarity and intent translation.

FAILURE MODE
Activity continues, direction degrades, no one names it.

WHAT YOU OBSERVE	PROBABLE CAUSE	GO TO
Divisions cannot connect daily work to the strategic end state.	Intent communicated as tasks without purpose or end state. The DTOF sequence is broken.	Ch. 1, 5
Team has objectives but no theory of how the approach produces the outcome.	A plan, not a strategy. Ends defined without ways.	Ch. 2
Everything is a priority. Resources spread across too many objectives without any being adequately resourced.	Failure to choose what NOT to do. No strategic editing.	Ch. 2

Method: treat the first match as a hypothesis. If the diagnosis does not improve conditions, look upstream.

Strategy & Direction

DOMINANT DEMAND
Strategic clarity and intent translation.

FAILURE MODE
Activity continues, direction degrades, no one names it.

WHAT YOU OBSERVE	PROBABLE CAUSE	GO TO
Strategy unchanged for a week despite changing conditions. Failures attributed to weather.	Team is not iterating. The plan has become the mission. Adaptation indicators ignored.	Ch. 7
Tactical actions succeed but strategic picture deteriorates. Activity confused with progress.	Tactics not advancing strategy. Outputs measured instead of outcomes.	Ch. 2, 9
Bold statements about priorities, no specificity about what / with what / by when.	Rhetoric substituting for strategy. Strategy test (specific enough to be wrong) not applied.	Ch. 2

Cross-references: for symptoms that may originate upstream, see Decision-Making (Ch. 4) and Communication (Ch. 5).

Decision-Making

DOMINANT DEMAND
Decision quality, independent of outcome.

FAILURE MODE
Delay disguised as prudence; consensus disguised as evaluation.

WHAT YOU OBSERVE	PROBABLE CAUSE	GO TO
Decisions consistently delayed. Team asks for more information when sufficient information exists.	Decision inertia. Culture evaluates on outcome, making deciding feel dangerous.	Ch. 4
One person's preferred option adopted without genuine evaluation of alternatives.	Advocacy mode, not inquiry. Process ratifies a preferred option rather than evaluating.	Ch. 4
Decisions justified by RMA products or remote analysis without field validation.	Illusion of analytical completeness. Proxies treated as ground truth. Distance from the field treated as objectivity.	Ch. 4

Method: treat the first match as a hypothesis. If the diagnosis does not improve conditions, look upstream.

Decision-Making

DOMINANT DEMAND
Decision quality, independent of outcome.

FAILURE MODE
Delay disguised as prudence; consensus disguised as evaluation.

WHAT YOU OBSERVE	PROBABLE CAUSE	GO TO
'Local knowledge' accepted without scrutiny. The word 'never' appears in operational assessments.	Authority of experience without scrutiny of evidence. Source weighted over content.	Ch. 4
No one has challenged the plan. Every head nods in the planning meeting. Dissent is absent.	Groupthink. Conditions for honest challenge do not exist.	Ch. 3, 7
Good outcomes celebrated without examining process. Bad outcomes trigger blame.	Decision quality being evaluated on outcome, not process. Asymmetric rigor.	Ch. 4, 7

Cross-references: weak decisions often follow weak Communication (Ch. 5) and weak Cognitive Readiness (Ch. 11).

Communication & Coordination

DOMINANT DEMAND
Intent that survives translation across levels and time.

FAILURE MODE
Shared understanding fragments; teams operate on different versions of reality.

WHAT YOU OBSERVE	PROBABLE CAUSE	GO TO
Division supervisors call for guidance on conditions they can see and assess themselves.	Centralized control disguised as coordination. Initiative suppressed.	Ch. 1
Tasks assigned in meetings but fall through the cracks. No one follows up.	Loops not closed. Tasks lack identified owners, deadlines, reporting.	Ch. 5
Divisions adapt to conditions but do not communicate the change. Other elements caught off guard.	Deviation without communication. Principle that deviation increases reporting requirements not followed.	Ch. 1, 5

Method: treat the first match as a hypothesis. If the diagnosis does not improve conditions, look upstream.

Communication & Coordination

DOMINANT DEMAND
Intent that survives translation across levels and time.

FAILURE MODE
Shared understanding fragments; teams operate on different versions of reality.

WHAT YOU OBSERVE	PROBABLE CAUSE	GO TO
Briefings are long but divisions leave without shared understanding of priorities.	Briefings are information dumps, not communication tools. Intent not communicated.	Ch. 1, 5
Team communicates certainty about outcomes they cannot control. Public trust erodes.	Language not calibrated to uncertainty. Confidence communicated that does not exist.	Ch. 4, 5
Vague criticism circulates. People feel blamed but no specific feedback is given.	Passive-aggressive communication. Direct, specific feedback being avoided.	Ch. 5, 7

Cross-references: communication failures both cause and reveal Team Performance issues (Ch. 9).

Team Performance & Cohesion

DOMINANT DEMAND
Trust as operational enabler — not value statement.

FAILURE MODE
Competence without coordination; tolerance becomes culture.

WHAT YOU OBSERVE	PROBABLE CAUSE	GO TO
Team competent individually but uncoordinated collectively. Communication formal and guarded.	Lacks shared mental models and trust. Ad hoc assembly without cohesion-building.	Ch. 8
When a decision produces a bad outcome, the response is 'we all decided.'	Accountability diffusion through collective language. Decisions lack identified owners.	Ch. 4, 8
A leader's behavior is erratic, abusive, or self-serving — and is being tolerated.	Counterproductive leadership not being addressed. Team sees what is tolerated.	Ch. 8

Method: treat the first match as a hypothesis. If the diagnosis does not improve conditions, look upstream.

DOMAIN 4 OF 7 · 2 / 2

Team Performance & Cohesion

DOMINANT DEMAND
Trust as operational enabler — not value statement.

FAILURE MODE
Competence without coordination; tolerance becomes culture.

WHAT YOU OBSERVE	PROBABLE CAUSE	GO TO
Team avoids difficult conversations. Feedback absent or delivered only as praise.	Niceness prioritized over fairness. Culture does not support honest challenge.	Ch. 7, 8
Team members disengaged. Assignment treated as routine regardless of complexity.	Complacency from under-matched assignment, or fatigue-driven disengagement.	Ch. 9, 10
New members struggle to integrate. Standing-team dynamics close ad hoc members out.	Onboarding not deliberate. Trust hierarchy rewards tenure over capability.	Ch. 9

Cross-references: team failures often originate in Mission Command (Ch. 1) and AAR culture (Ch. 8).

Planning & Adaptation

DOMINANT DEMAND
Proactive posture and planning horizon discipline.

FAILURE MODE
Team plans for the past or executes through the present without adapting.

WHAT YOU OBSERVE	PROBABLE CAUSE	GO TO
Team has no contingency plans, or contingency plans cannot be implemented in time available.	Contingency planning is afterthought. Triggers, timelines, resources not specified. Time test fails.	Ch. 7
Same plan executed day after day. Midday update and post-ops debrief produce no changes.	Daily cycle has become ritual. Iteration not occurring. Meetings as habit, not tool.	Ch. 5, 6
Conditions have clearly changed but strategy has not. Failures attributed to external conditions.	Anchored to plan. Sunk cost, confirmation bias, ego preventing adaptation.	Ch. 4, 6

Method: treat the first match as a hypothesis. If the diagnosis does not improve conditions, look upstream.

Planning & Adaptation

DOMINANT DEMAND
Proactive posture and planning horizon discipline.

FAILURE MODE
Team plans for the past or executes through the present without adapting.

WHAT YOU OBSERVE	PROBABLE CAUSE	GO TO
AARs conducted but nothing changes. Lessons identified but not implemented.	Gap between lessons identified and lessons learned. Stewardship failure (p. 87).	Ch. 7
Reports describe what happened in terms that match the plan rather than what occurred.	Gap between work as done and work as reported. Honest reporting does not feel safe.	Ch. 7
Detailed plans for day 7 with the same precision as plans for tomorrow.	Planning beyond what is knowable. Cognitive resources invested in fiction. Planning horizon broken.	Ch. 7

Cross-references: adaptation failures often surface as Strategy & Direction issues (Domain 1).

Cognitive & Human Factors

DOMINANT DEMAND
Human limits as predictable constraints on judgment.

FAILURE MODE
Cognitive depletion produces decisions that look reasonable but are not.

WHAT YOU OBSERVE	PROBABLE CAUSE	GO TO
Leaders working 16–18 hr days and dismissing concerns about rest. Briefing and decision quality declining.	Fatigue worn as a badge of honor. Leader degrading their own instrument.	Ch. 10
A leader fixates on one problem or data point while other relevant information goes unaddressed.	Tunnel vision from cognitive overload or fatigue. Attentional narrowing under sustained demand.	Ch. 10
Practices unacceptable on day one are routine by day ten. No one named when it shifted.	Normalization of deviance. Standards eroded incrementally without deliberate decision.	Ch. 3, 10

Method: treat the first match as a hypothesis. If the diagnosis does not improve conditions, look upstream.

Cognitive & Human Factors

DOMINANT DEMAND
Human limits as predictable constraints on judgment.

FAILURE MODE
Cognitive depletion produces decisions that look reasonable but are not.

WHAT YOU OBSERVE	PROBABLE CAUSE	GO TO
Team going through the motions. Energy low. Humor and connection have disappeared.	Sustained operations without recovery or meaning reinforcement. Belonging eroded under load.	Ch. 9, 11
Decisions increasingly made by the most senior person. Subordinates stop offering alternatives.	Authority bias amplified by fatigue and stress. Cognitive depletion defaults to hierarchy.	Ch. 1, 3, 10
Leader confident in projection (Level 3 SA) but cannot articulate the comprehension (Level 2) supporting it.	SA built on weak comprehension. Projection failure waiting to happen. Endsley levels collapsed.	Ch. 11

Cross-references: cognitive degradation underwrites every other domain. Treat it as the upstream cause when others repeat.

Evaluation & Development

DOMINANT DEMAND
Measuring capability rather than compliance.

FAILURE MODE
System rewards what is easy to measure, not what the environment requires.

WHAT YOU OBSERVE	PROBABLE CAUSE	GO TO
Evaluations are generic. 'Meets expectations' is the default with no specifics.	Evaluation lacks behavioral anchors. System measures compliance, not capability.	Ch. 10
Leaders who have only operated on low-complexity incidents express confidence in readiness for high complexity.	Dunning-Kruger. Self-assessment calibrated to a simpler environment than they will face.	Ch. 10
System prioritizes standardized configurations over demonstrated capability.	Uniformity valued over effectiveness. Cannot distinguish compliance from competence.	Ch. 10

Method: treat the first match as a hypothesis. If the diagnosis does not improve conditions, look upstream.

Evaluation & Development

DOMINANT DEMAND
Measuring capability rather than compliance.

FAILURE MODE
System rewards what is easy to measure, not what the environment requires.

WHAT YOU OBSERVE	PROBABLE CAUSE	GO TO
Successes celebrated without examining whether process was sound. Failures investigated; successes are not.	Asymmetric rigor. Success reinforces unexamined assumptions. Luck mistaken for skill.	Ch. 4, 7
Generous evaluations across the board. Distinctions disappear. No actionable feedback.	Evaluation system optimized for harmony, not improvement. The next incident reveals the gap.	Ch. 10
Punitive evaluations make difficult assignments career risk. People take the safer path.	Evaluation measures who took the safer route, not who built the harder capability.	Ch. 10

End of Diagnostic Index. Section V (Rapid Strategy Screen) follows.

SECTION V

Rapid Strategy Screen

20 questions. 15–30 minutes. A go / no-go check at every major decision point.

The Screen is the operational instrument. It does not tell you what to think. It surfaces what the team has not yet examined — assumptions, single points of failure, tradeoffs accepted by default rather than on purpose.

A clean screen is not a guarantee. A failed screen is a warning.

USE AT

Strategy approval
Before committing to a strategy or significantly modifying one.

Objective changes
When incident objectives change or a new delegation arrives.

Major decision points
Transitions between management strategies, Type transitions, demobilization.

Conditions materially change
Weather events, significant fire behavior, resource drawdown, political shifts.

SEVEN CLUSTERS — TWENTY QUESTIONS

A · Framing & End State	Q 1 – 3
B · Assumptions & Evidence	Q 4 – 6
C · Constraints, Tradeoffs & Alternatives	Q 7 – 9
D · Risk & Vulnerability	Q 10 – 12
E · Feasibility & Execution	Q 13 – 15
F · Adaptation & Learning	Q 16 – 18
G · Decision Quality	Q 19 – 20

PARENT REFERENCE
OLFG Appendix B, pages 305–316.

RELATED CHAPTERS
Ch. 2 (Strategy) · Ch. 3 (Red Teaming) · Ch. 4 (Decision Quality)

TWO TIERS · ENTRY POINT AND FULL INSTRUMENT

Match the Screen to the Time

THE PRINCIPLE

Six questions when minutes are short. Twenty when there is room
for the full check. Both surface the same categories of vulnerability —
the deeper instrument tests each category more thoroughly.

TIER 1 · ENTRY POINT
Six Strategic Questions · 5 minutes

USE WHEN

Time is compressed. Radio call.
Quick check before a hand-off.
Initial screen before a deeper review.

WHAT IT CATCHES

- Wrong problem being solved
- Undefined success
- Unexamined opportunity cost
- Unexamined alternative
- Logic leap rather than link
- Unidentified single point of failure

WHAT IT DOES NOT CATCH

Assumption fragility, evidence quality,
tradeoff specifics, execution feasibility,
adaptation triggers, challenge culture.

WHERE IT LIVES

Ch. 3 (p. 54). Available everywhere
the Companion travels.

*Use the six even when time permits
the twenty — as a warm-up.*

TIER 2 · FULL INSTRUMENT
Rapid Strategy Screen · 15–30 minutes

USE WHEN

Time permits a structured check.
Strategy approval, transition,
or material change in conditions.

WHAT IT ADDS

- Assumption testing and evidence
- Risk accepted on purpose vs. by default
- Second- and third-order effects
- Decentralization boundary
- Adaptation triggers
- Challenge structure (who is heard)

SCORING

Green / Yellow / Red / Unknown.
Load-bearing items marked ★.
Scoring detail on next page.

WHERE IT LIVES

Section V (pp. 124–130).
Full version in parent OLFG App. B.

*Same categories as the six — deeper
testing in each category.*

*A clean Tier 1 screen permits action. A failed Tier 1 screen
demands the Tier 2 review before commitment.*

SCORING · WHAT THE SCREEN PRODUCES

How to Score

THE LESSON

Four scores. Each carries a different operational signal.
Scoring is honest about what is known, what is assumed, and
what cannot be answered yet. Mark UNKNOWN, do not guess.

GREEN	**Answered with evidence and confidence.** Move forward. Document the evidence supporting the answer.
YELLOW	**Answered, but with significant uncertainty.** Note the uncertainty. Test it during execution. Revisit at next decision point.
RED	**Cannot answer, or answer reveals a critical gap.** Stop and resolve before commitment. Generate an output (p. 130).
UNKNOWN	**Insufficient information to assess.** Assign an owner and a deadline. Mark in the assumptions register.

LOAD-BEARING QUESTIONS · MARKED ★

Six questions in the Screen are marked load-bearing (★). These test
categories where a failure is most likely to collapse the strategy:

- Q4 / Q5 / Q6 — Assumption identification, fragility, evidence calibration.
- Q10 / Q12 — Single point of failure; risk accepted on purpose.
- Q14 — Where decentralization actually applies.
- Q20 — Whether challenge is permitted and heard.

THE STOP RULE

If more than five questions score RED or UNKNOWN — and any are load-
bearing — the strategy is not ready for approval without explicit risk acceptance.

QUESTIONS 1 - 7 · 1 / 3

Framing & Assumptions

1	What problem are we actually solving — and what problem are we accidentally solving instead?	**A**
2	What does success look like in observable, measurable terms (end state), and by when?	**A**
3	What values are in tension (life safety vs. tempo, cost vs. effectiveness, suppression vs. resource benefit)?	**A**
4	What are the top three assumptions this strategy depends on?	**B** ★
5	Which assumption is most fragile — and how will we test it in the next operational period?	**B** ★
6	What evidence supports this strategy — and what evidence would change our mind?	**B** ★
7	What are the non-negotiable constraints (policy, safety, legal, agency direction, political)?	**C**

CLUSTER KEY · ★ MARKS LOAD-BEARING

- **A** Framing & End State
- **B** Assumptions & Evidence
- **C** Constraints, Tradeoffs & Alternatives
- **D** Risk & Vulnerability
- **E** Feasibility & Execution
- **F** Adaptation & Learning
- **G** Decision Quality

QUESTIONS 8 - 14 · 2 / 3

Tradeoffs & Risk

8   What are we optimizing for — and what are we willing to trade?   `C`

9   Compared to the best alternative strategy, why is this one better? (One sentence.)   `C`

10   What single point of failure could collapse this strategy?   `D` ★

11   What are the likely second- and third-order effects (displacement, cascading impacts, resource draw)?   `D`

12   What risk are we accepting on purpose, and is it prudent relative to the objective?   `D` ★

13   What does this strategy require from the field that the system may not reliably deliver?   `E`

14   Where must decisions be pushed to field leaders — and what decisions stay centralized?   `E` ★

CLUSTER KEY · ★ MARKS LOAD-BEARING

A   Framing & End State
B   Assumptions & Evidence
C   Constraints, Tradeoffs & Alternatives
D   Risk & Vulnerability
E   Feasibility & Execution
F   Adaptation & Learning
G   Decision Quality

QUESTIONS 15 - 20 · 3 / 3

Execution & Adaptation

15 Is intent clear enough that division supervisors can act correctly when the plan breaks? — E

16 What are the trigger points that force us to adapt, reinforce, or reverse course? — F

17 What is our minimum viable path to progress in the next 24–72 hours? — F

18 If this strategy fails, what will we wish we had done earlier? (One-minute premortem.) — F

19 What activity is consuming resources without plausibly advancing the intent (line to nowhere)? — G

20 Who has explicit license to challenge this strategy — and how will that challenge be heard without penalty? — G ★

CLUSTER KEY · ★ MARKS LOAD-BEARING

A Framing & End State
B Assumptions & Evidence
C Constraints, Tradeoffs & Alternatives
D Risk & Vulnerability
E Feasibility & Execution
F Adaptation & Learning
G Decision Quality

WHEN THE SCREEN SURFACES RED

Outputs

THE LESSON
Any RED or UNKNOWN item that matters generates one or more
of three outputs. They integrate with strategic assessment processes
and create the trail for real-time decisions and after-action learning.

01 ASSUMPTIONS REGISTER

Assumption · evidence supporting it
Method to test it · owner · deadline
Threshold for action

Each field carries a deliverable. Owners and deadlines are mandatory.

02 DECISION LOG

Decision made · rationale
Dissenting views captured
Triggers for revisiting

Each field carries a deliverable. Owners and deadlines are mandatory.

03 RISK TRADEOFF NOTE

Risk accepted · why
What was gained by accepting it
Conditions making the tradeoff unacceptable

Each field carries a deliverable. Owners and deadlines are mandatory.

USE THE EXPANDED CHECK WHEN

- The Screen surfaces multiple RED or UNKNOWN items.
- Extended attack or complex incident transitions where strategic
  quality is high-consequence.
- Preparing strategic assessments for agency administrators.

Full Expanded Planning Quality Check in parent OLFG Appendix B, Part 2.

END OF SECTION V

The Screen is a discipline, not a verdict. The strategy is yours.
The Screen surfaces what your team has not yet examined. Appendices follow.

APPENDIX A

DEBrIEF Detail

After-action review — step by step.

The structure that turns lessons identified into lessons learned.
Each step has a purpose; skipping any step degrades the process.
The lowercase "r" is intentional — chronological review is the
least valuable part. The learning lives in the other steps.

Insights that exist only in memory have a half-life measured in days.

IN THIS APPENDIX

Psychological Safety — the precondition
An AAR conducted where people are afraid to speak honestly
is not an AAR. It is a performance.

D + E — Define and Engage
Set duration and objectives. Create conditions for honest
participation. The leader goes first with a real mistake.

B + r — Background and review
Preparatory aspects. Validated assumptions. Then the
chronological review — the least valuable part.

I + E — Internal and External reflection
Individual reflection. Then team. One thing done well,
one thing to improve. Specific. Actionable.

F — Follow-up that produces change
Where most AARs fail. Insights acknowledged, nothing changes.

Questions That Go Deeper
Beyond the steps — what the team is not yet ready to say.

THE PRINCIPLE

If the AAR produces ten recommendations and none
are assigned, the AAR was a conversation.
Not a learning event.

PARENT REFERENCE
OLFG Ch. 8, pages 180–212.

RELATED CHAPTERS
Ch. 8 (AAR & Learning) ·
Ch. 9 (Team Cohesion)

THE NON-NEGOTIABLE PRECONDITION

Psychological Safety

THE PRINCIPLE

An AAR conducted in an environment where people are afraid
to speak honestly is not an AAR. It is a performance — a recitation
of acceptable observations that avoids the uncomfortable truths
that are the actual source of learning.

WHAT IT IS

Shared understanding that honest mistakes — errors made in good
faith while attempting to execute the mission — are treated as
learning opportunities rather than evidence of incompetence.

WHAT IT IS NOT

Absence of accountability.

Safety enables honesty. It does not exempt anyone from
responsibility for what they did or did not do.

HOW IT GETS BUILT

- **The leader goes first.** With a real mistake, specifically described.
  Not a rehearsed anecdote. The team needs to see honesty practiced, not performed.

- **Demand specifics.** "We communicated well" — about what, with whom, when?
  Generalities produce the feeling of reflection without the substance of it.

- **Close the gap between work as done and work as reported.**
  If reports match the plan rather than what happened, the problem is the culture.

- **Assign accountability for follow-up.** Insight without ownership decays.
  Each recommendation gets an owner by name, with a deadline, before the AAR ends.

- **Treat consequences proportionally.** To action, not to outcome.
  A sound decision that produced a bad outcome is not the same as a reckless one that got lucky.

*Psychological safety is a culture, not a form. Built through daily action —
not invoked at the start of a meeting.*

STEPS 1 & 2 · SET CONDITIONS

Define & Engage

DEFINE

PURPOSE

Set a clear timeframe before the AAR begins —
10 minutes, 30 minutes, 2 hours.
Outline the objectives of the response being reviewed.

HOW

Anchor the discussion to what was supposed
to happen. Without this anchor, the AAR
drifts into general discussion rather than
structured analysis.
Without defined duration: ends prematurely
or drags until counterproductive.

Tells participants how detailed their contributions need to be.

ENGAGE

PURPOSE

Create the conditions for honest participation.
The leader shares a personal mistake to
normalize discussing errors.

HOW

This is not a warm-up. It is the deliberate
establishment of the conditions under which
the rest of the AAR will either produce
insight or produce nothing.
If engagement is low, the facilitator must
diagnose why — almost always: safety not built.

Demonstrate honesty is safe by being honest first. Specifically. Vulnerably.

STEPS 3 & 4 · SHARED UNDERSTANDING

Background & review

BACKGROUND

PURPOSE

Review the pre-incident and preparatory aspects.
Was the necessary preparation completed?
Was the plan clear?
Were dependencies and assumptions validated?

HOW

This step focuses on the non-operational
aspects — the conditions that existed before
execution began.
Problems identified here are systemic rather
than tactical. Often the highest-leverage
learning points — they affect every subsequent
decision.

Pre-incident gaps cascade into every operational period that follows.

review

PURPOSE

Analyze the execution chronologically.
What happened and why — without yet addressing
future improvements.

HOW

Lowercase r is intentional. The chronological
timeline is the LEAST valuable part of the AAR.
Teams default to timeline recitation because
it is safe and factual. But knowing WHAT
happened is not learning.
Build shared understanding of what occurred,
not evaluate it. Evaluation comes later.

The timeline is a scaffold, not the structure. Learning lives in why, not when.

Internal & External

INTERNAL

PURPOSE

Individual reflection.
One thing each person did well.
One thing each person would do differently.

HOW

Specific. Actionable.
Generalities don't help anyone learn —
demand specifics.
'I need to improve my decision-making' is not
actionable. 'I should have surfaced the
weather change to the IC at 1400 instead
of 1600' is.

Each person owns their reflection. The team learns by hearing it spoken.

EXTERNAL

PURPOSE

Team reflection.
Coordination across positions, handoffs,
interactions with external partners,
communication with adjacent functions.

HOW

Same specificity requirement.
'Coordination with Air was good' is not useful.
'The handoff at shift change skipped the
TFR boundary update — the night team operated
for two hours on stale airspace info' is.
External patterns are systemic — fix the
system, not just the individual.

Individual learning compounds when team patterns are surfaced and named.

STEP 7 · WHERE MOST AARs FAIL

Follow-up

FOLLOW-UP THAT PRODUCES CHANGE

What needs to happen after the debrief to apply the learning.

Most AARs fail here. Insights are acknowledged in the room, then nothing changes. The team executed a ritual rather than a learning event.

For learning to outlive the team, it must be captured in transferable form.

WHAT FOLLOW-UP REQUIRES

A NAMED OWNER FOR EACH RECOMMENDATION
Before the AAR ends. Not "the team" or "leadership." A person by name.

A DEADLINE
Specific date. "By next ops period." "By the end of the assignment." "By the next AAR."

A DEFINITION OF DONE
How will the team know the change has happened? An observable outcome —
not "discussed at next meeting."

PERSISTENCE BEYOND THE TEAM
Changes to processes, tools, documentation that persist after demobilization.
Learning that lives only in heads disappears when the heads rotate out.

REPORTING BACK
At the next AAR or planning session, status of prior recommendations is reviewed.
If the team sees follow-up tracked, they invest in honest input. If they don't, they don't.

THE STOP RULE FOR AAR FACILITATORS

Do not adjourn the AAR until every recommendation has a named
owner and a deadline. Unowned recommendations are not
recommendations. They are aspirations.

WHAT STANDARD REVIEWS MISS

Questions That
Go Deeper

THE LESSON

The DEBrIEF steps produce structured learning. These questions
surface insights that standard reviews miss — and tend to surface
what the team is not yet ready to say.

WHAT WAS THE GREATEST RISK WE TOOK AND GOT AWAY WITH?

Calibrates the team's understanding of risk and reveals
near-misses that would otherwise go unexamined.

Most teams have one. Surfacing it changes risk calibration for the next assignment.

IF WE HAD UNLIMITED RESOURCES, WHAT WOULD WE DO DIFFERENTLY?

Separates resource constraints from strategic and process
limitations. Resource constraints often mask other failures.

If the answer is 'the same thing,' the constraint was never the real problem.

IF THE PLAN FAILED, WHERE WOULD IT FAIL?

Surfaces the failure mode the team is closest to but not
yet talking about. The premortem applied retroactively.

Ask even when the plan succeeded — especially when it did.

WAS THAT SOUND PROCESS — OR WAS THAT LUCK?

Ask after every favorable outcome. If you cannot distinguish,
you are building future performance on foundation you do not understand.

Process is what you control. Luck is what you got. Confuse them and you run the same play again.

*These questions surface the human factors that influence decision quality —
but rarely appear in operational reviews.*

APPENDIX B

Fatigue Detail

Stress, sleep, and cognitive readiness.

Performance impairments to be managed through discipline,
planning, and leadership — not subjective experiences to be
managed through motivation.

This is not a wellness chapter. It is a performance chapter.

IN THIS APPENDIX

Acute vs. Chronic Stress
Acute stress mobilizes; chronic stress depletes. Day one
leader is not the day ten leader.

Dopamine Buffer · Immune Window
Why morale is physiological, not soft. Why people get sick
after the crisis ends — not during it.

Fatigue — The Impairment You Cannot See
Fatigue degrades the cognitive function needed to recognize
fatigue. Self-assessment becomes unreliable.

Operational Targets
Sleep, environment, and recovery — managed inputs, not
aspirational targets.

Cognitive Load — Three Types
Intrinsic · Extraneous · Germane. Where to attack, where
to protect, where to match capability.

Symptoms of Cognitive Overload
In yourself first. In the team second.

THE PRINCIPLE

A fatigued leader does not just feel tired. They make worse
decisions, communicate less clearly, fixate on irrelevant
information, and lose the cognitive flexibility complexity demands.

PARENT REFERENCE
OLFG Ch. 11, pages 253–278.

RELATED CHAPTERS
Ch. 9 (Team Cohesion) ·
Ch. 11 (Cognitive Readiness)

PHYSIOLOGY · TWO REGIMES

Acute vs. Chronic Stress

THE LESSON

Stress is designed to move you. Acute stress — adrenaline-based —
is short-term by design. Wildfire assignments are not short-term.
They are the domain of chronic stress.

THE SHIFT — ADRENALINE TO CORTISOL

ACUTE STRESS · ADRENALINE-BASED MOBILIZATION

Enhances immune surveillance. Sharpens attention. Accelerates reaction time.
An asset when the demand is intense and brief.
Time-limited crises. The first hours of an incident. Acute structure protection.

CHRONIC STRESS · CORTISOL-BASED ENDURANCE

Sustained acute response shifts the body from mobilization to endurance.
Prolonged elevated cortisol suppresses immune function, degrades memory
consolidation, impairs cognitive flexibility.

Reduces capacity for nuanced, context-dependent thinking — what complexity demands.

THE DAY-ONE LEADER IS NOT THE DAY-TEN LEADER

The leader who arrives sharp and energized may be cognitively
impaired by day ten — not from lack of discipline, but because
physiology has been depleted by sustained demand without
adequate recovery.

This is not a question of toughness. It is biology operating as designed.
The countermeasures are physiological too — addressed on the next page.

The body is built for acute stress. It is not built for sustained operations.
The discipline that protects performance must come from leadership.

TWO PHYSIOLOGICAL FACTS

Dopamine Buffer
& the Immune Vulnerability Window

THE DOPAMINE BUFFER — WHY MORALE IS PHYSIOLOGICAL

Dopamine — the neurochemical of reward, meaning, and purpose —
pushes back against epinephrine burn rate and restores capacity
to sustain effort.

WHAT GENERATES IT

- Humor.
- Gratitude expressed specifically.
- Recognition of progress, named.
- Connection to purpose, restated.
- Social bonds within a cohesive team.

These are not soft leadership activities.
They are physiological countermeasures to the neurochemical
depletion that degrades performance.

THE IMMUNE VULNERABILITY WINDOW

Early in the stress response, immune function gets a boost —
evolutionary adaptation for potential injury during fight-or-flight.

Later, when the acute phase ends and the body shifts into
recovery, immune function is suppressed.

WHY THIS MATTERS OPERATIONALLY

People get sick AFTER the crisis ends — not during it.
The period immediately after demobilization is a vulnerability window.

*A workforce chronically depleted between assignments is less capable
on the next one. The bill comes due, even when no one sees it on the fire.*

A leader who maintains morale is not being nice.
They are maintaining the cognitive capability of their team.

THE IMPAIRMENT YOU CANNOT SEE

Fatigue

THE LESSON

Fatigue is the most pervasive and least addressed cognitive impairment in incident management. It is invisible to the leader experiencing it — and that is the operational problem.

WHAT THE RESEARCH SHOWS

ACUTE SLEEP LOSS

After 17–24 hours without sleep, cognitive performance degrades to levels equivalent to a blood alcohol content of 0.05–0.10%.

CHRONIC RESTRICTION

5–6 hours nightly over multiple days — the norm on many wildfire assignments — produces cumulative impairment one good night does not resolve.

THE INSIDIOUS QUALITY

Fatigue impairs the cognitive functions needed to recognize impairment.

Fatigued leaders believe they are performing adequately because their self-assessment capability has been degraded by the same fatigue degrading their performance.

They do not notice the narrowed attention, the slowed processing, the increased fixation on irrelevant details, or the reduced capacity for creative problem-solving.
They feel like they are performing — and they are wrong.

WHAT TO DO — TRUST THE TEAM, NOT YOURSELF

- When your self-assessment is degraded, the team's assessment of you is more reliable than your own. Ask. Listen. Trust their reading.

- Build safety-critical decisions on the night shift around two-person concurrence.

- A rested deputy outperforms a depleted commander. Delegate before the breaking point.

NOT ASPIRATIONS · CONTROLS

Operational Targets

THE LESSON

These are not aspirational targets. They are operational controls
that directly affect the cognitive capability of the people making
decisions on your incident.

DOMAIN	OPERATIONAL TARGET
SLEEP	**7-9 hr daily when possible** Tactical naps 20–30 min when not. Pre-deployment sleep banking.
NOISE	**< 40 dB outside · ~30 dB inside** Separate sleeper camps from ICP. Enforce quiet hours. Relocate generators.
LIGHT	**Pre-sleep: dim & amber** Avoid blue light before sleep. Red/amber light in sleep zones.
AIR	**PM2.5 as low as practicable** HEPA in tents and indoor sleepers. CO monitors. No idling near sleep areas.
TEMPERATURE	**60-67°F where feasible** Cool sleep environments improve deep sleep. Target where possible.
CAFFEINE	**200-400 mg/day max** Cutoff 6–8 hr pre-sleep. Strategic use — not constant.
RECOVERY	**Predictable R&R into rotations** Two-person concurrence for safety-critical calls on night or beyond 12 hr on duty.

Every target is within the leader's control. Every one is routinely neglected.
Cognitive readiness is a system the leader operates — not a value they hold.

WHEN THE SYSTEM EXCEEDS THE PROCESSOR

Cognitive Load — Where to Attack

THE LESSON

Cognitive overload occurs when volume and complexity of information, decisions, and coordination demands exceed processing capacity. Stress and fatigue amplify it. A well-rested leader can still be overwhelmed.

01 INTRINSIC
Inherent to the task

Complex incident with multiple divisions, changing weather, competing stakeholder demands carries high intrinsic load.

MATCH

Cannot be reduced. Match it to capability through training and exposure. Distribute it through clear delegation.

02 EXTRANEOUS
Imposed by the system

Unclear briefings. Redundant meetings. Poorly designed forms. Micromanagement. Conflicting direction.

ATTACK

This is the leverage point. System-imposed waste that adds no value. Cancel meetings not synchronizing. Simplify briefings.

03 GERMANE
Builds capability

Pattern recognition. Mental models. Schema. Productive processing that converts information into insight.

PROTECT

Reserve time and attention for this. Reflective practice. Red teaming. The cognitive work of becoming a better leader.

Every centralized decision that could be delegated, every unclear briefing — extraneous load on leaders who can least afford it.

WHEN INTRINSIC + EXTRANEOUS LOAD EXCEEDS CAPACITY

Symptoms of Cognitive Overload

THE LESSON

When intrinsic + extraneous load exceeds capacity, predictable failure patterns appear. Recognize them in yourself first — fatigue degrades the same self-assessment that should be flagging them.

IN YOURSELF — RECOGNIZE FIRST

- **Tunnel vision** — fixation on one problem while others go unaddressed.

- **Freezing** — inability to act despite continued engagement.

- **Loss of SA Level 3** — reacting, not anticipating.

- **Working harder, accomplishing less** — effort decoupling from output.

If you cannot recognize these symptoms in yourself, the team can. Ask them.

IN THE TEAM — OBSERVE SECOND

- **Briefings degrading** — long, less synthesized, more recap.

- **Decisions deferred upward** that previously stayed at the right level.

- **Errors in routine tasks.** Communication shortcuts that drop precision.

- **Quality of work degrading** while reported hours unchanged or increased.

Team symptoms appear before individual symptoms in many cases — watch the team.

WHAT TO DO — REDUCE LOAD

Cancel meetings not synchronizing. Simplify briefings.
The leader's job is not to be busy. It is to be effective.

Decision Triggers

When to act, reset, or transfer.

The trigger conditions for the decisions a leader makes by exception. Pre-defined so the moment is recognized when it arrives — not constructed under load.

A trigger pre-committed in calm is a trigger you can act on in chaos.

IN THIS APPENDIX

Revisit · Inflection · Reset
When to revisit the strategy. When to call an inflection point.
When to reset standards before drift becomes culture.

Escalate · Transfer · Demobilize
When to escalate beyond delegated authority. When to
transfer command. When to begin demobilization planning.

Trigger Practice
Three failure modes for triggers — and how to address each.
Re-evaluation under stress is how organizations ratify inertia.

THE PRINCIPLE

The decision was made when the trigger was defined.
The moment when the trigger fires is just the execution
of a decision already made.

PARENT REFERENCE
OLFG Ch. 1 (Decision Elevation), Ch. 7 (Adaptation Triggers).

RELATED CHAPTERS
Ch. 4 (Decision Quality) ·
Ch. 7 (Contingency)

Revisit · Inflection · Reset

When the strategy needs reexamination — and when standards need reset.

REVISIT THE STRATEGY WHEN

- Fire behavior repeatedly exceeds the containment concept.
- Resource picture deteriorates below minimum required.
- Stakeholder priorities shift in ways the strategy does not accommodate.
- Key assumptions proven wrong — and the plan still depends on them.
- Tactical actions succeed while the strategic picture deteriorates.

CALL AN INFLECTION POINT WHEN

- Conditions have shifted enough to invalidate the strategy, not just adjust it.
- Continuing exposes personnel for an end state no longer achievable.
- The cost of changing direction is now lower than the cost of continuing.

RESET STANDARDS WHEN

- PPE compliance has slipped from explicit to implicit.
- Briefing standards on day eight differ from day one.
- Practices unacceptable on day one are normal by day ten.

Revisit is adjustment. Inflection is replacement. Reset is restoration.

AUTHORITY · COMMAND

Escalate · Transfer · Demobilize

When the leader's authority must change — or be surrendered.

ESCALATE WHEN

- Decision exceeds delegated authority — life safety, jurisdiction, financial, political.
- Required resources are not available within delegated channels.
- Strategic guidance from agency administrator is unclear or unavailable.
- The decision will be visible to political or media oversight.

TRANSFER COMMAND WHEN

- Complexity has increased beyond the current team's qualification.
- Personal cognitive readiness is degraded to a level that affects judgment.
- Continuity of leadership through the next operational period cannot be assured.

BEGIN DEMOBILIZATION PLANNING WHEN

- Strategic objectives are within reach in the planning horizon.
- Resource requirements are stable or declining.
- Transition to a smaller organization is feasible without losing capability.

Escalation protects the system. Transfer protects the mission. Demobilization protects the team.

Trigger Practice

THE LESSON

Triggers fail in three ways: not defined in advance, defined but not monitored, monitored but not acted on. Each failure mode has a different cause — and a different repair.

01 NOT DEFINED IN ADVANCE

CAUSE

Triggers feel speculative until conditions change.

REPAIR

Include trigger definition as a required output of the planning process. No plan ships without them.

02 DEFINED BUT NOT MONITORED

CAUSE

No one owns watching for the condition.

REPAIR

Assign monitoring explicitly — by name, with reporting cadence and escalation path.

03 MONITORED BUT NOT ACTED ON

CAUSE

Psychological cost of acting feels higher than continuing.

REPAIR

Pre-commit to the action when the trigger fires. The decision was made when the trigger was defined.

The leader's discipline: when the trigger fires, act.
Re-evaluation under stress is how organizations end up ratifying inertia.

APPENDIX D

Strategic Questions

Six Questions · Four Ways of Seeing.

Structured challenges for stress-testing operational plans.
Use at the front end of strategic thinking — before the
assumptions check, before the premortem.

The cheapest red team is the one you run before commitment.

IN THIS APPENDIX

Six Strategic Questions

Six questions to ask before committing to a strategic
direction. Each surfaces a different category of vulnerability.
Tier 1 entry point to the Rapid Strategy Screen.

Four Ways of Seeing

Examine the plan from four distinct perspectives.
Each surfaces blind spots the others cannot.
The gap between any two views is information.

WHEN TO USE

Six Strategic Questions

Strategy approval, objective changes, operational period transitions,
when conditions materially change. 5 minutes.

Four Ways of Seeing

When the plan feels airtight and you need to test the assumption that
others see what you see. Before transitions. Before stakeholder briefings.

PARENT REFERENCE
OLFG Ch. 3 (Red Teaming).

RELATED
Section V (Rapid Strategy Screen)

TIER 1 ENTRY POINT · STRESS-TEST BEFORE COMMITMENT

Six Strategic Questions

THE LESSON

Six questions to ask before committing to a strategic direction.
Each surfaces a different category of vulnerability. Skip any one
and the corresponding category remains untested.

1

PROBLEM DEFINITION

*What problem are we solving — and what problem
are we accidentally solving instead?*

2

OUTCOME CLARITY

*What does success look like in observable,
measurable terms — and by when?*

3

OPPORTUNITY COST

*What are we choosing not to do — and what
does that choice cost us if we are wrong?*

4

ALTERNATIVE TEST

*Compared to the best alternative strategy, why
is this one better? (One sentence.)*

5

LOGIC AUDIT

*Where does the logic of this strategy depend
on a leap rather than a link?*

6

FAILURE MODE

*What single point of failure could collapse this
strategy — and what is our response if it does?*

*Skip any one — and the corresponding category of vulnerability remains untested.
Six is the entry point. The Rapid Strategy Screen (Section V) is the deeper instrument.*

FOUR PERSPECTIVES · WHAT A SINGLE VIEW MISSES

Four Ways of Seeing

THE LESSON

Examine the plan from four distinct perspectives. Each surfaces
blind spots the others cannot. Used in sequence, the four reveal
what a single viewpoint always misses.

HOW WE SEE OURSELVES

The plan as we have written it.
Our intent, our capabilities, our reasoning.
The view from inside the planning tent.

Familiar. Coherent. Less informative than it feels.

HOW WE SEE THEM

Our assessment of the conditions, the fire,
the stakeholders, the agency administrator,
the public.

The view we have constructed of others.

HOW THEY SEE US

How the agency administrator, the public,
the cooperating agencies, the affected
community see our team and our approach.

Often different from the planning-tent view.

HOW THEY SEE THEMSELVES

How the other actors understand their own
situation, priorities, constraints, and intent.
The view from inside their tent —

rarely what we assume from outside.

THE PRINCIPLE

The gap between any two views is information.
The largest gaps are usually the highest-leverage learning.

INDEX · 1 / 3

Framework Index

Framework Index

INDEX · 3 / 3

Framework Index

FRAMEWORK / TOOL	LOCATION
Trust as Enabler (3 dimensions)	Ch. 9
Standing vs. Ad Hoc Teams	Ch. 8
Counterproductive Leadership (4 categories)	Ch. 8
Fairness Over Niceness	Ch. 8
Two Opposing Evaluation Failures	Ch. 9
Dreyfus Model · Novice to Expert	Ch. 9
Behaviorally Anchored Scales	Ch. 9
Capability vs. Compliance	Ch. 9
Endsley SA Model · 3 Levels	Ch. 10
Cognitive Load Types (Intrinsic/Extraneous/Germane)	Ch. 10, App. B
Normalization of Deviance	Ch. 10
Five-Phase Leadership Arc	Section II
Diagnostic Index (7 domains)	Section IV
Rapid Strategy Screen (20 questions)	Section V
Decision Triggers	Appendix C
Decision Quality Five Criteria	Inside Back Cover

Five Criteria

A high-quality decision has all five. Use these before commitment as a check; use them after as a frame for the AAR.

01 PROBLEM CLARITY

A clearly defined problem — and confidence the right problem is being solved.

02 STATED ASSUMPTIONS

Load-bearing assumptions identified, challenged, and tested.

03 GENUINE EVALUATION

Real alternatives evaluated — not ratification of one option.

04 VERIFIABLE REASONING

Reasoning the team can verify and challenge.

05 OWNERSHIP & TRIGGERS

An owner by name, and triggers that would cause the decision to be revisited.

EVALUATE DECISIONS INDEPENDENT OF OUTCOMES

The wind shifts. The radio fails. The forecast misses.

Process is what you control. Outcome is what you get.
Confuse the two and you will run the same play expecting a different result.

Before I Act

The framework you reach for first is a habit, not a decision. Under pressure, speed, fatigue, or conflict, every leader defaults to something.

These are not prompts to fill in. They are questions to ask yourself — in the truck, on the walk to the briefing, before the read hardens into a plan.

You cannot challenge a default you have not named.

THE CONTROL DEFAULT — AM I TIGHTENING MY GRIP?

— Am I centralizing because the situation demands it, or because I am uncomfortable with uncertainty?
Asking for updates to build shared understanding is orientation. Asking to regain personal control is not.

— What decision should stay with the person closest to the problem?
Pulling decisions upward when consequences are visible is the most common way mission command quietly dies.

THE SPEED DEFAULT — AM I MOVING BEFORE I UNDERSTAND?

— Am I acting on the first workable explanation?
The first read that fits is rarely the only read that fits. Premature closure feels like decisiveness.

— What am I treating as fact that is only an assumption? Who sees this differently?
Name the assumption out loud. If no one in the room disagrees, you may not have the right room.

THE EXPERIENCE DEFAULT — AM I FIGHTING THE LAST INCIDENT?

— What past event is shaping how I see this one — and where is this one meaningfully different?
Pattern recognition is fast and usually right. The danger is forcing a pattern that does not fit.

THE RELATIONSHIP DEFAULT — AM I AVOIDING FRICTION?

— Am I accepting weak information because I trust the source? Am I leaving the group unchallenged to protect cohesion?
Trust speeds you up and can blind you. Who has not spoken yet?

Before I Decide

Run this before a major decision, a deviation from the plan, or a recommendation you are about to commit to. It is a bias interrupter, not a delay.

Shared understanding is not everyone quietly agreeing. It is built through disciplined challenge.

WHAT AM I ASSUMING?

— State the assumption plainly — then ask what evidence would prove it wrong.
Not what supports it. What would break it, and who can verify it before the decision is made.

WHAT AM I OVERWEIGHTING?

— Which input is carrying more weight than it has earned?
The most recent update · the loudest voice · the original plan · the person with rank · the easiest metric to measure.

WHAT AM I UNDERWEIGHTING?

— What am I discounting because it is quiet, inconvenient, or slow to measure?
Weak signals · field-level concerns · fatigue · resource limits · community impact · second- and third-order effects.

WHAT IF I AM WRONG?

— If my current read is wrong, what is the first indicator I will see — and what trigger changes my course?
A decision with no trip-wire is a decision you have stopped watching. Name the condition that makes you reassess.

WHO GETS A DISSENT VOTE?

— Before I finalize, who have I asked to challenge this — and do they have permission to?
Disciplined initiative requires someone empowered to say the read is wrong. Name them. Ask them. Then decide.

Free enough to adapt. Disciplined enough to stay aligned with intent.

9 798999 590562 2